SPEAKEASY

SECRET BARS AROUND THE WORLD

WHITE STAR PUBLISHERS

SPE⚷KEASY

SECRET BARS AROUND THE WORLD

Text by
MAURIZIO MAESTRELLI

Project Editor
LAURA ACCOMAZZO
VALERIA MANFERTO DE FABIANIS

Graphic Design
PAOLA PIACCO

CONTENTS

Preface by Samuele Ambrosi   6

Introduction   8

The Noble Experiment   12

Always better than nothing...   22

Speakeasies...of today   32

The Back Room – New York City   38

Employees Only – New York City   42

PDT (Please Don't Tell) – New York City   46

Raines Law Room – New York City   50

Dear Irving - New York City   54

Le 4e Mur – Montreal   56

The Violet Hour – Chicago   58

Williams & Graham – Denver   60

Circa 33 – Portland   66

Bourbon & Branch – San Francisco   70

The Laundry Room – Las Vegas   74

The Del Monte Speakeasy – Los Angeles   78

Noble Experiment – San Diego   82

Jules Basement – Mexico City   86

Eau de Vie – Sydney   92

Bar Nayuta – Osaka   98

Ounce – Taipei   102

001 – Hong Kong   104

Foxglove – Hong Kong   106

The Blind Tiger – Yangon   110

The Speakeasy – Athens   116

L'Antiquario – Naples   120

Jerry Thomas Project – Rome   124

Malkovich – Genoa   130

Mad Dog Social Club - Turin   136

1930 – Milan   140

The Parlour - Frankfurt   144

Die Rote Bar – Frankfurt   146

Reingold – Berlin   148

Becketts Kopf – Berlin   150

Drip Bar – Hamburg   152

Door 74 – Amsterdam   154

The Butcher – Amsterdam   158

Jigger's – Ghent   160

Cahoots - London   162

Evans & Peel – London   168

Callooh Callay – London   170

Nightjar – London   174

The Blind Pig – London   182

Moonshiner – Paris   186

Little Red Door – Paris   188

Le Syndicat – Paris   190

Lavomatic – Paris   194

Paradiso – Barcelona   198

A Brief Speakeasy Glossary   202

My Speakeasies   204

Biographies - Acknowledgments   206

PREFACE

The long friendship I have enjoyed with the author of this book began in 2008 at an international Calvados competition that I won with one of my cocktails. Our friendship is built on mutual esteem, dialogue and a common passion for the art of drink mixing that binds us, albeit in different roles. Over time, we have become a reference point for each other, and now I have been asked to go on record with a few considerations. I am happy to comply because the story of modern speakeasies is a story of success based on one fundamental element. Mystery. All of today's speakeasies are concept bars that reproduce the secrecy and privacy of their historical counterparts without necessarily copying the most characteristic features of the period which, quite honestly, were not that inviting. Often, they were located in makeshift settings like cellars or basements, and the drinks were usually made with any kind of alcohol the proprietor was able to procure, sometimes from bootleggers or, worse, moonshiners. One product in particular that was popular during Prohibition comes to mind–Peeko, a concentrate that could be flavored to taste like rye whiskey, rum, gin, cognac or vermouth. Gin was the most difficult flavor to achieve and sometimes required adding turpentine or sulfuric acid. Not exactly the healthiest of elements. Obviously, Peeko was used in the working-class speakeasies; certainly not in the luxurious ones whose patrons included members of high-society, the authorities and entertainment celebrities.

But Prohibition era America produced one good thing, at least for Europeans. When bars closed down, many of the great American bartenders relocated to the Old Continent and brought their knowledge of mixed drinks with them. Without their fundamental contribution of recipes, techniques, liquors and spirits, bartending would not be what it is today.

But today? What does the term speakeasy mean today? Secrecy, even though, naturally, it is never absolute, passwords and access codes, hard to find addresses . . .

All of this seems to indicate that what counts more than anything in modern speakeasies is the experiential aspect which, in my opinion, is not enough. During my career, I have had the occasion to visit a number of speakeasies around the world and often, once I had found the venue and reached the goal of getting in, I was disappointed. Because these elements have to be part of the experience, not the whole experience. A speakeasy is not excellent just because it is hidden in another business or because it requires an extremely difficult password to get in; it has to be exciting and noteworthy. Excellence comes not only from the secrecy and privacy of the location, but also from the atmosphere, a warm reception, and an appreciation, both of the products and the techniques necessary to create the aromas and flavors of the cocktail you will soon be holding.

Samuele Ambrosi

Head Barman and owner of the Cloakroom Cocktail Lab in Treviso (Italy)

Winner of numerous international competitions and

BarMaster and BarAcademy instructor

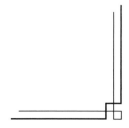

INTRODUCTION

"Our country has deliberately undertaken a great social and economic experiment, noble in motive and far-reaching in purpose."
Herbert Hoover, 31st President of the United States of America

There seems to be an inextricable connection between the Prohibition era and certain Hollywood movies. From Brian De Palma's "The Untouchables" to Sergio Leone's "Once Upon a Time in America", alcohol is a regular feature, along with the clandestine establishments that served it and the Irish and Italian-American gangsters who frequented them. But there was a lot more than that to the years of the Prohibition era, which lasted almost 14 years, from January 16th, 1920 when it entered into effect until December 5th, 1933 when it was abolished. The ban on producing, distributing and selling alcohol throughout the entire nation had grave economic consequences; those who had labored in the industry found themselves suddenly unemployed, and the government lost large sums of tax revenues. There were social consequences as well, with an increase in alcohol related deaths, particularly among those who home-distilled their liquor with products that damaged their health.

But those years had some positive effects as well—consider the growing success of jazz, the increasing recognition in American society of the role of women, who were given the right to vote in 1920, and the Art Deco esthetics that spread through the world of art, architecture, and sculpture.

Speakeasies were frequented not just by gangsters, but also by entertainers, by the jet set, and by a large part of America's society at the time. They became a safety valve for that great number of Americans who considered Prohibition an unjustifiable infringement on their rights, including the right to drink, and who viewed the Eighteenth Amendment as a violation of the principles expressed in their Constitution signed in Philadelphia in 1787.

As the years passed after the repeal of Prohibition, the era and its characteristics, including of course the speakeasies, began to take on a kind of romantic glow. Bartenders all over the world have cultivated that glow—the fascination of secrecy and the forbidden, even if it is no longer the case; the vintage cocktails, some of which were invented long before the Prohibition era; and the low lights and adventurous atmosphere of the speakeasy—and they have turned it into a trend. A trend that has successfully brought the cocktail, and the creativity and talent of the bartenders who make it, back to center stage. Some of these speakeasies are difficult to find-hidden at the back of other establishments or in their basements. You need to know the password to get into some, and others require the answer to a question that changes every day. Still others are practically in plain sight, but maintain the aura and charisma of bygone speakeasies.

Some of them began as public establishments, became speakeasies during Prohibition, and then opened to the public again after Prohibition was abolished.

Each of the places described in these pages has a different story. But all of them have a story to tell.

Maurizio Maestrelli

• *Note: Not every establishment agreed to furnish the recipe for its signature cocktail, and some of those who did, indicated the ingredients without the exact amounts. Quite fitting since one of the charms of speakeasies is their desire to keep at least some of their "secrets" secret.*

THE NOBLE EXPERIMENT

*"When I sell liquor, it's called bootlegging; when my patrons serve it
on Lake Shore Drive, it's called hospitality."*

Al Capone, gangster

The news reached San Francisco on the afternoon of December 5th, 1933—Washington had
ratified the Twenty-first Amendment and Prohibition was finally over. The sirens on top of the
Ferry Building in the "City by the Bay" started wailing at 2:31 pm and shortly after, fourteen trucks
paraded up Market Street and stopped in front of city hall to "honor" the Italian-American mayor,
Angelo Rossi, with cases of California wine and gin.

According to legend, when President Franklin Delano Roosevelt signed the historical bill in the
Oval Office of the White House, his comment was: "I think this would be a good time for a beer".
An impressive crowd and a marching band greeted a load of alcoholic beverages arriving at the port
in Los Angeles. Prohibition had banned the production, distribution and consumption of alcohol for
over 13 years, and the day it ended was celebrated as a sort of Liberation Day.

Today, the word Prohibition brings to mind films like "The Untouchables" with Robert De
Niro as Al Capone and Kevin Costner in the role of the incorruptible Elliot Ness. Or Sergio Leone's
masterpiece "Once Upon a Time in America" or, more recently, the television series "Boardwalk
Empire", set in Atlantic City in the 1920s. The era of Prohibition made its appearance in literature
as well. It was the setting for many books, from Francis Scott Fitzgerald's "Great Gatsby" to Mario
Puzo's "The Godfather" and, over the years, Prohibition took on a kind of romantic aura, depicting
those who drank illegal alcohol as adventurous rebels. But Prohibition was much more than that, and
in many ways it was quite different from the phenomenon portrayed in books and movies. But how
could a law that so heavily infringed upon personal rights ever come to be enacted in a traditionally

10-11 • Celebrating the end of Prohibition in Chicago.
*13 • The Prohibition era marked the advent of the illicit, secret bars that became famously known
as "speakeasies". In New York alone there were over thirty thousand, many of which were not
as "secret" as they may have been thought to be.*

liberal country that was founded in the spirit of individualism? The answer to that question lies further back in the country's history.

For many years, alcohol had certainly occupied a role in American society. It all began in 1620 when the Pilgrims that had set sail from England aboard the Mayflower landed on the shores of today's Massachusetts. The ship's hold carried about forty-two tons of beer and ten thousand gallons of wine, and it almost certainly carried liqueurs and distilled spirits as well. Among the nation's founders there were a number of alcohol enthusiasts. George Washington distilled whiskey at his country estate and in his own words one needed nothing more than "a glass of wine and a bit of mutton" to be happy. Thomas Jefferson was responsible for having grape vines planted in Virginia and his own wine cellar was well stocked with over twenty thousand bottles of French wine. The important social role taverns played in America's earlier years confirm that the consumption of alcohol was a part of daily life. Taverns were a place for everyday socializing, but they were also home to many of the political meetings that would shape the country's history. In fact, it was at the Indian Queen Tavern in Philadelphia with a glass of Madeira on the table that Jefferson began writing the Declaration of Independence, and New York's first City Hall was actually located in a tavern in lower Manhattan. That is not to say that alcohol consumption was excessive or unregulated at the time. In the 1600s the British colonies had already begun to adopt measures to limit overdrinking. There were laws that regulated opening and closing times of taverns and laws that imposed fines on both the proprietor who served alcohol to a drunk patron and on the patron who had had too much to drink. It is true, however, that in the era of Washington and Jefferson there were already those who harshly criticized drinking alcohol. Benjamin Rush was a professor of medicine at Pennsylvania University and was one of the signers of the Declaration of Independence. He began warning against the dangers of alcohol in 1774, and ten years later he wrote an article containing a list of all of the risks inherent to its excessive consumption. His opinion was accepted and promoted by other luminaries and particularly by a number of religious leaders. To cite one verified example, in 1786 the Quaker Church of New England ordered all of its members to quit drinking distilled spirits. And so began the long road to Prohibition called the "Temperance Era", temperance meaning the abstinence from alcohol. Throughout the 19th century in American society, the demands for reform that were championed by the Temperance Movement grew stronger, slowly but surely. Advocates included religious factions and women's leagues as well as manufacturers' and industrial associations.

The social and economic changes taking place in the United States in the 1800s helped strengthen the argument for reform. In fact, the waves of immigrants arriving from Italy, Ireland, Greece, Portugal and Poland were a primary source of tension in a society that was still in its youth. The new customs and traditions they imported along with their "different" religion—most of them were Catholic—created a social rift. The consumption of alcohol was an important part of many immigrant cultures, and Nativists used this as a way to distance themselves from the newcomers who were often looked upon with diffidence to say the least. The idea of frequenting taverns on a daily basis, which the immigrants did, became indecorous and reprehensible. The Protestant Church in many of its denominations was among the first to execrate alcohol and its consumption. The Evangelical Christians of the Second Great Awakening believed that the consumption of alcohol was "an evil force that threatened to destroy individuals and weaken society", and the Reverend Lyman Beecher preached that drinking was "a sin that was leading to the destruction of the nation".

This viewpoint became increasingly widespread during the 1820s and eventually led to the foundation of the Temperance Movement, which was a melting pot of various Temperance Societies. The first, the United States Temperance Union, was founded in Connecticut in 1789. The movement also included the American Temperance Society, which was founded in Boston in 1826 and 10 years later boasted nearly a million and a half members as well as the "Washingtonians", an association of ex-drinkers from the working class that had its roots in urban areas but rapidly spread throughout the entire country.

The weight of the Temperance Movement was soon tangible. Alcohol consumption per capita decreased dramatically between 1830 and 1845, and in 1851 Maine was the first state to ban the sale and public consumption of alcohol. A short time later, thirteen other states followed suit.

The ban stalled when the Civil War broke out in 1861. Some states reversed their previous decision to uphold it, but as soon as the conflict was over the campaign to defeat alcohol regained momentum, stronger than ever. Among the organizations to join the movement was the Woman's

Christian Temperance Union (WCTU) which was founded in Ohio in 1873 and became one of the first feminine grassroots movements. The WCTU was unlike other organizations in that it actively boycotted establishments that served alcohol. Initially, its members limited their protest to singing religious hymns outside of the taverns and saloons, but later they resorted to rolling liquor barrels into the streets in front of the establishments and smashing them to pieces. The Women's Crusade contributed to the closing of around thirty-one thousand saloons between 1873 and 1874. The Prohibition Party had been founded a few years earlier, in 1869, with the intent of transforming the anti-alcohol petitions into a political battle. Although the party nominated its candidates in every presidential election since 1872, it had little tangible success. It was nonetheless able to exercise its influence on the Republican Party, which slowly began to join the cause for prohibition.

Another wave of immigration at the end of the 19th century, together with rapidly increasing urbanization, stoked social tensions once again, the result of which was an expansion of the Temperance Movement and the foundation of what was to be considered the most incisive prohibition association—the Ohio Anti-Saloon League, founded in 1893 by Howard Hyde Russell. The organization rapidly spread throughout the nation and owed its strength, at least in part, to a number of distinguished industrial magnates that sponsored it, including John D. Rockefeller, the president of the Standard Oil Company, and Henry Ford, who declared that "the speed of our motors, of our machinery and of our lives in general is incompatible with alcohol consumption."

Russell's organization played a decisive role in the Prohibition battle. In 1906 only six states had enacted legislation prohibiting the sale of alcohol, but just six years later that number had increased to ten. Even before Prohibition had become law, about half of the country's population lived in territories where alcohol was banned. A Constitutional Amendment prohibiting the consumption of alcohol was first proposed in 1914, and although it was defeated by Congress, its approval was only a question of time. When the United States joined the fighting in World War I, the consumption of alcohol decreased even more and the national beers whose production had primarily been in the hands of German immigrants were boycotted.

In August, 1917, the decision was made to ban all alcohol production for the duration of the war in order to preserve grain stocks, and in 1918 Congress approved the Eighteenth Amendment that prohibited the production, sale and transportation of alcoholic beverages throughout the nation.

President Woodrow Wilson's veto of the bill was overridden, and the amendment was approved on October 28th, 1919. The Volstead Act, which provided enforcement for the amendment, was enacted and on January 16th, 1920 Prohibition became the law.

It was the beginning of what President Herbert Hoover called the "Noble Experiment"—thirteen incredible (though not necessarily positive) years that were ushered in in a variety of manners. On the evening of January 15th, a wealthy patron of New York's Park Avenue Hotel held a grand party to say goodbye to alcohol where a coffin was filled with bottles and the orchestra played funeral dirges until midnight. In New Orleans, a gentleman named Walter Parker built two new cellars in his house and furnished them with more than five thousand bottles of wine. Mary Pickford's mother filled the alcohol void by buying a liquor store's entire stock. But for all of the other Americans who treated themselves to an occasional drink, times were about to get difficult. And not only for them, as Prohibition meant that all of the activities surrounding the production and sale of alcohol would close and all of the workers involved would face unemployment. Breweries and distilleries closed, as did bars and saloons. The companies that transported alcohol went bankrupt. Thousands of people had to look for new employment. At the same time, the part of the population that had no intention of giving up alcohol began to take countermeasures. It is difficult to say what motivated them—the appeal of alcohol, the desire to defend their individual rights or the idea of a business opportunity— but many Americans were committed to finding a way to get alcohol back into circulation.

Bootleggers prospered, smuggling alcohol from Canada, Mexico, and the Caribbean, and illegal distilleries flourished, producing "moonshine" in outdoor stills under the light of the moon. Other homemade "distilleries" used bathtubs to mix alcohol with other ingredients. The alcohol used in these concoctions often came from cosmetic products that contained modest quantities, such as aftershave lotions and shampoos, and the result was a beverage that was dangerous and sometimes even fatal.

The incidence of liver cirrhosis caused by alcohol abuse decreased during the first years of Prohibition, but it was not long before the tendency was completely reversed. Organized crime saw a great opportunity for profit. It took over the illegal trafficking of alcohol and the network of speakeasies, those hidden establishments that would go down in history. The Prohibition era was a time when alcohol, gambling and prostitution brought millions of dollars a year to gangsters like

Al Capone, Lucky Luciano, Johnny Torrio, Bugsy Siegel and Dutch Schultz. Another well-known name was that of Enoch "Nucky" Johnson, a politician-cum-crime boss who controlled Atlantic City and guaranteed that it remained an "alcohol oasis" during those years.

It soon became glaringly obvious that the ban would not resolve the problems related to alcohol abuse on its own; rather, it multiplied them and actually created new ones. In New York alone, the fifteen thousand bars in existence prior to Prohibition became nearly thirty-two thousand speakeasies. Seven years after the enactment of Prohibition, deaths caused by the consumption of dangerous liquor and spirits numbered in the tens of thousands. Cases of blindness and paralysis caused by homemade spirits were rampant, and the crime rates that the supporters of Prohibition thought would diminish, actually increased. Burglaries increased 13.2%, homicide by 16.1%, and robbery by an incredible 83.3% as corruption spread through the local police forces, politicians and even among federal agents. Last but not least, States soon realized that closing bars and distilleries had meant losing a substantial amount of revenue. Research

• *Membership cards to various establishments and, on the right, the entrance to a speakeasy. The peep-hole was used to observe potential clients in order to decide whether to let them in.*

puts the loss of revenue during Prohibition at around eleven billion dollars nationally, while the cost of enforcing the ban has been calculated to be about 300 million dollars. With these numbers in mind, the tide that had led to the enactment of Prohibition in 1920 began to ebb. Just as associations had been founded to promote Prohibition, associations to repeal it began to arise—associations of both men and women. In some cases, authoritative exponents that had supported Prohibition changed their minds. The winds began to shift as The Great Depression of 1929 put a severe strain on American society, and the importance of potential jobs related to the alcohol industry became more evident. The Democratic Party had always showed a certain indifference to Prohibition, but its pledge to repeal it became one of Franklin Delano Roosevelt's

• *Prohibition was never able to take alcohol completely out of circulation. A certain tolerance was always demonstrated in upper class haunts and restaurants, sometimes because they were frequented by public officials and politicians.*

strongest presidential campaign promises in 1932. After Roosevelt's election, Prohibition's days were numbered. Voiding the amendment was not easy. A favorable vote by three quarters of the States was necessary, but on December 5th, 1933, in Utah, the Twenty-first Amendment that put an end to Prohibition was fully ratified. Each State was given the authority to regulate matters concerning alcohol and some chose to continue to uphold the ban, but for the vast majority of Americans, December 5th, 1933 marked the return to legally producing, transporting, selling and drinking alcohol. The Twenty-first Amendment essentially decreed the failure of Prohibition politics, putting an end to an era and giving birth to the legend of those incredible thirteen years of American history and to the legend of the speakeasies.

• *The inside of a speakeasy on New York's East Side in 1932.*
Since many secret bars were controlled by organized crime,
Prohibition came to be associated with the era of gangsters.

ALWAYS BETTER THAN NOTHING . . .

"They say that the British can't fix anything properly without a dinner,
but I'm sure the Americans can't fix anything without a drink."

Frederick Marryat ("Diary in America", 1839)

There is one phrase that sums up the spirits (both alcoholic and philosophical) of the Prohibition era better than most, and it came from Will Rogers, an American actor and comedian from the 1920s. He said: "Prohibition is better than no liquor at all".

To think that Americans would stop drinking alcohol just because the Eighteenth Amendment and the Volstead Act prohibited it was already proving to be preposterous in the years immediately following the ratification of the amendment.

While it is true that the amount of alcohol consumed per capita decreased radically, particularly at the beginning of the 1920s, it is also true that the illegal production and sale of alcohol, often in the hands of organized crime, flourished as did the gimmicks for finding a drink without getting caught by the police.

One of the effects of Prohibition was the radicalization of social inequality—the rich were able to circumvent the ban, on one hand, by buying up huge amounts of spirits and liqueurs before it went into effect, and on the other, by travelling to countries where alcohol was still legal. Canada, Mexico and the Caribbean saw a remarkable increase in popularity during what may have been the first instances of "mass" tourism. Crossing the border into Canada for a drink or two became commonplace for those who could afford it. Being only ninety miles from Florida, Cuba was easy to reach by motor boat, and Havana soon became known as the Paris of the Caribbean. Pan Am Airlines saw a chance to profit from "Cuban weekends" and soon began organizing direct flights between Key West and Havana. In fact, it is estimated that in 1921, about 275,000 passengers flew to Cuba on a regular basis. In an attempt to put an end to the phenomenon, a Prohibition leader invoked the Monroe Doctrine, which established American supremacy over the entire continent, and even called for a military intervention into the island. But it certainly could not be said that Prohibition was being respected by everyone everywhere in the homeland either. In New York, for example, a beverage

• *A wooden crate for a stool, although a well-furnished bar was all these four friends needed.*

similar to beer, in fact surprisingly similar to beer according to customers, continued to flow at McSorley's Old Ale House, and New Orleans soon became famous as a kind of paradise where almost no one respected the ban. The Old Absinthe House (which still stands in Bourbon Street today) advertised that it "appeared to be the only establishment that did not sell spirits". The irony of the claim was obvious.

Prohibition in the United States was a boon for the producers of alcoholic beverages abroad. Canada had actually lived its own period of Prohibition at the beginning of World War I, but after 1918 each single province was given the choice to continue upholding the ban or not. Quebec immediately chose to legalize the production of liquors and spirits again. British Columbia followed suit in 1920, and Ontario and Alberta did the same in 1924. Much of the alcohol produced was destined to the United States and as Harry Hatch, president of the Canadian distillery Hiram Walker, said: "The Volstead Act does not in any way prohibit us from exporting our products. It prohibits those on the other side of the border from importing them. There is a difference". Another Canadian company called the Mexican Export Company claimed that it exported its products to Mexico and Cuba through the United States. Obviously, not a single bottle reached its final destination, which was not surprising since both Mexico and Cuba were home to manufacturers with their own interests in supplying alcohol to the American market.

Soon after Prohibition came into effect, hundreds of taverns that were often managed by Americans popped up just across the northern and southern borders. At the same time, the bars of the great luxury hotels in Havana began living their moment of glory. They were patronized every weekend by the American jet set, as well as by the organized crime bosses whose arrogance and haughtiness helped create the atmosphere that was a prelude to the future rebellion led by Fidel Castro.

A great deal of alcohol entered the United States despite the Volstead Act, and just as much was produced within the country's borders. The less affluent who could not afford drinking weekends in Havana or Mexico or Canada were forced to drink illegally produced alcohol or to make their own. The government's ban was defied by the clandestine distillers or "moonshiners" that spread throughout the rural areas of the country and the producers of "bathtub gin" which referred to any alcoholic beverage produced at home, often in the bathtub.

- *On the left, a woman demonstrates how to transport bottles of liquor without arousing suspicion. On the right, port, peach brandy, gin, absinthe and other types of liquor bring a smile to the face of this woman photographed in a speakeasy. Upper class establishments always offered a wide choice of beverages . . .*

Whether it was imported or produced nationally, all of this alcohol ended up in someone's glass. The best, most expensive products could be found at the private parties of the wealthy, whereas the ones produced with slipshod or even dangerous methods and ingredients ended up in low-level, illegal establishments or were imbibed at home.

Even the world of the speakeasies was somehow divided according to social classes. The more important clubs, like the Stork Club or the 21 Club, both in New York, enjoyed total protection that was sometimes furnished by the police. In fact, the 21 Club opened in 1922 under the name of The Red Head and changed location often, becoming more and more exclusive, but it always kept a table reserved for the local Chief of Police. Generally speaking, the alcohol served in these establishments was good, but there were exceptions.

The writer Heywood Broun narrated an experience he had one evening at the El Fey, another famous New York club that was managed by a former actress, Texas Guinan. Since he was there on a first date and wanted to make an impression, Broun decided to order champagne, but Guinan, who was a friend of his, warned him that even though it would cost him thirty dollars, he would be getting a cheap imitation and suggested he order gin instead. So, yes, cheap liquor was served in luxurious clubs, too. In fact, many authors claim that cocktails became such a great success during Prohibition because adding fruit juices and sodas to cheap alcohol masked its unpalatable flavor.

• Some members of the Women's Christian Temperance Union shattering confiscated barrels of liquor. Female religious associations were fundamental in promoting and supporting Prohibition.

There is no doubt that the success of the speakeasies had one common denominator—alcohol—in whatever way, shape or form it was served. Straight up or mixed, it was all imbibed. Many of the cocktails that were popular before the Prohibition era continued to be favorites even when served with illegal alcohol. Some of them are still fashionable today and others are just being rediscovered.

Jerry Thomas is often considered the father of mixed drinks in America. In 1862 he published his book, "The Bar-Tender's Guide". It was the first book about cocktails ever published in the United States, and it made many cocktails famous before the Prohibition era. The Martinez, for example, was a kind of "forefather" and almost certainly inspired the more famous Dry Martini, also popular before the 1920s, and the Tom Collins, invented in London at the end of the 1800s. One of the cradles of the cocktail was New Orleans, where the Sazerac was a favorite—a mix of cognac, sometimes substituted with rye whiskey, absinthe, a sugar cube and two drops of Peychaud's Bitters. The Ramos Gin Fizz, invented by Henry Ramos in 1880, was also popular. Harry MacElhone, the barman at what was to become the legendary Harry's New York Bar in Paris, published his book, the "ABC of Mixing Cocktails" in 1922. The book contained nearly 400 recipes and is a good indication of what was being served on either side of the ocean at the time. It included recipes for cocktails that are still fashionable today, such as the Alexander, the Americano, the Bronx, the Clover Club, the Daiquiri (that was erroneously printed as Dacquari in the book), the Gibson, the Gimlet, the Gin Rickey, the Manhattan,

• Under the watchful eye of police officers, confiscated whiskey is poured into the sewer in a New York City street.

the 75 (which later became famous as the French 75, named after a French artillery piece used during World War I) and the Sidecar, just to mention a few.

The Englishman Harry Craddock was another barman who became famous during that period. A naturalized American citizen, he worked at the Knickerbocker Hotel in New York, but returned to London as soon as Prohibition began. In 1930, when he was already at the helm of the legendary American Bar in the Savoy Hotel, he published "The Savoy Cocktail Book" that contained over 750 recipes. Even though it is impossible to describe all of them, some deserve particular attention. One of the most interesting is the Mary Pickford, named for an actress who was very famous at the time and who was also, quite probably, an enthusiastic drinker. The actress was born in Canada, but became such an American sensation that she was referred to as "America's Sweetheart". Her fame equaled that of Charlie Chaplin, the actor with whom she co-founded United

• On the left, after raiding one of the many speakeasies that came into being in the era of Prohibition in the United States, two plain-clothes police officers try to determine the origin of the bottles of alcohol confiscated from the basement.

• Two agents inspect the more than five hundred bottles of homemade beer seized when the police from the 15th Precinct raided a speakeasy in Rockaway Beach, New York.

Artists film studios. When she visited Cuba in 1922 with her husband Douglas Fairbanks, another famous actor of the era, Fred Kaufman, the bartender at the bar of the Sevilla Hotel, served her a cocktail with light rum, maraschino, fresh pineapple juice and grenadine syrup that he named after her. From Cuba, the cocktail quickly traveled to the United States and was soon found in the very best American speakeasies.

It is clear that during the era of Prohibition the art of mixing drinks thrived despite the risk of exposure to alcohol that was cheap or even a health risk. But for the most part, the quality of the speakeasies patronized by the jet set was guaranteed, and today you can find a number of classifications of the most popular cocktails of the period. The Spirits Business, an authoritative voice on the subject, places the Mary Pickford in the top ten along with the Gin Rickey, a favorite of Francis Scott Fitzgerald, author of "The Great Gatsby". Rum, which was initially the basis for this cocktail, was replaced by gin during Prohibition, given its greater availability. Other historical cocktails that gained their position in the top ten during those "prohibitive" years include the Mint Julep, which became even more famous in this period; the French 75; the Tom Collins, which was also made popular by the ready availability of gin, though in its milder version; the Sidecar; the White Lady; the Whiskey Sour and the Bees Knees, whose ingredients, including honey and lemon juice, did an excellent job of covering the taste of even the worst bathtub gin. Last but not least is the Bacardi Cocktail, which owes its popularity to the ease with which the Cuban-produced Bacardi Rum illegally made its way to the shores of North America.

Outside of the circle of high-class speakeasies were the establishments known by another nickname— blind pig or blind tiger. These were frequented by lower social classes, and the mixed drinks served there were most often limited to distilled spirits diluted with fruit juice—cranberry was very popular—or with non-alcoholic beverages like cola or lemonade. On one hand, this was a way to mask the defects of "craft" alcohol, and on the other, mixing such drinks required little talent or know-how on the part of the bartender. They also required very little time—something which was useful if the police happened to show up.

Regardless of the type of alcohol—distilled spirits, beer, wine or cocktails, Prohibition proved that a government ban was not enough to quench the Americans' desire to drink. There are many authors who assert that this desire was not so much a need for alcohol or for a break from work or family commitments as it was a more general rebellion against the infringement on personal freedoms that the Eighteenth Amendment introduced into the Constitution of the United States. An infringement that the majority of the American population found unacceptable and successfully rebelled against, bringing an end to Prohibition in 1933.

• 1928: American actor Wheeler Oakman, as gangster 'Hawk' Miller, peers through
a slit in the door of a Broadway speakeasy in a still from "Lights of New York."

SPEAKEASIES . . . OF TODAY

What is left of the speakeasies of the 1920s? "Nothing", we might say, since it is now perfectly legal to produce, sell and drink alcohol in every country in the world. Well, in reality, this is not the case. There are some areas of the United States that are divided into "dry counties" and "wet counties". In the dry counties, the sale of alcohol is still regulated in varying degrees. One example is Tennessee. It may be the home state of the famous Jack Daniel's Distillery, but the sale of whiskey in public establishments is prohibited. An exception was made for the store of the distillery, probably to meet the demands of the thousands of visitors each year, but that is the extent of it; they are allowed to buy one celebratory bottle to take home. Kansas and Mississippi are also dry, and it is estimated that 10% of the American population lives in areas where strict laws regulate the sale or the consumption of alcohol. In some counties of Mississippi, the mere transportation of alcohol is prohibited.

Obviously, the difference in laws from place to place exists because each single state in the Union, and not the Federal Government, establishes policies regarding alcohol. That the subject continues to be relevant almost a century after the abolition of Prohibition is emblematic. In any case, in 1933, the speakeasy phenomenon ended and all of the activities surrounding the legal sale of alcohol were quickly revived. But the fascination with the secrecy and the forbidden nature of speakeasies must have taken hold. It is the only explanation for the success of today's speakeasy-themed establishments that are back in fashion, not only in the United States, but all over the world.

Many of today's speakeasies or secret bars are actually very difficult to find, and apparently the proprietors themselves seem in no hurry to divulge their exact locations. Many of them are hidden within other businesses—from coin laundries to antiques shops to gentlemen's haberdasheries to hamburger and taco bars, just to mention a few. They are often without any kind of sign outside their door, and some have a spy-hole that allows the doorman to verify the identity of potential customers before opening the door for them. In some places, a password that changes frequently is required to get in, and at others hopeful patrons must send a text message and wait for a reply before they are admitted. In other words, a good part of the allure of these clubs resides in respecting the rules of secrecy, at least from the outside, and

34-35 • A crowded speakeasy in 1932.

in the fact that the clubs themselves are hidden from the gaze of ordinary passersby. But the success of the speakeasy "style" goes hand in hand with the art of drink mixing, which in recent years has made a remarkable comeback. The bartender has become a truly creative alchemist who mixes up potions that can thrill, shock, or maybe soothe the adrenaline after a hard day's work. It all depends on the recipe he chooses to fill your cocktail glass.

Liqueurs and distilled spirits are back in fashion, and homemade products like syrups, extracts, and freshly-squeezed fruit juices have found their place in the world of mixology. Professionally made ice that is as transparent as a cut diamond is popular, too. Sculpted by patient, talented hands, the finished product may be diamond-shaped or it may be a sphere. There are the classic cocktails, sometimes with a personal twist, but often exactly as they were originally conceived—the quintessential drinks that often have their roots in a time that preceded even the Prohibition era. It is a veritable renaissance fueled by the study of the faithful, "sacred" texts of mixology from the books of Jerry Thomas and Harry MacElhone to the legendary "Savoy Cocktail Book" that Harry Craddock published in 1930, while Prohibition was in full swing.

The joy of joys of the speakeasy revival is the return of capable bartenders. They know how to convey all the craftsmanship of their profession to even the most industrially distilled spirits, skillfully transforming them in cocktails with their talent and flair. And they do it under the watchful eye of the customer, exactly like bartenders did almost two hundred years ago. In today's speakeasies, the pace is slow, measured in sips that keep consumption within the limits of enjoyment, company and gratification; a quicker pace might spoil the pleasure and turn it into an ugly, senseless experience. The revival of speakeasies also contributed to the return of a number of musical genres that had been all but forgotten—the old Delta blues from Mississippi, traditional jazz, ragtime and swing. Sounds that turn back time to the 1920s, to the Roaring Twenties; years when, despite Prohibition, the desire to experiment and the zest for life and transgression were expressed by a generation that had survived a world war and that, unknowingly, would soon have to face yet another.

In reality, the return of speakeasies has the nostalgic flavor of those faraway years when hope was in the air . . . and in the drinks.

36-37 • The entrance to the Back Room in New York.

THE BACK ROOM

A visit to The Back Room is a walk down memory lane that conjures up visions of the Hollywood movie stars and New York theater actors that regularly crossed its hidden threshold. It evokes memories of the likes of Lucky Luciano, Bugsy Siegel and Meyer Lansky who met up there for "business meetings" and who knows, maybe shared a bottle of Champagne. The Back Room was a real speakeasy in the 1920s. It was one of the few in New York City that operated during Prohibition and is still in existence today. Its name was slightly different then; it was called The Back of Ratner's. And Ratner's was a famous Jewish kosher restaurant. The door is still the same, the ambiance reflects the original style and atmosphere and patrons still sip their cocktails from teacups just as they used to do. In the day, it gave a veil of secrecy to the kind of beverages they were drinking and, at least for a moment, might have tricked the public officials who frequently raided the speakeasies.

It is no surprise that The Back Room is one of the regular stops on New York's "speakeasy tour" or that it appears in such popular television series as "Boardwalk Empire" and "Secrets of New York". It is an ideal setting for a movie with tapestries on the wall, plush red velvet armchairs and sofas, big mirrors behind the bar, carpets, paintings and antique radios on the mantle. Its reputation draws a crowd and even though patrons only need a password to get in on Monday nights when there is live jazz music, reserving a table in advance is advised. Minors under 21 are not admitted during the week, and patrons must be 25 or older to get in on Friday and Saturday. The Back Room organizes and hosts private parties as well, and even though celebrities still often frequent The Back Room, none of them are the "dangerous" gangster types of yesteryear.

102 Norfolk Street, New York City, USA
Telephone: +12122285098
backroomnyc.com

Hidden from the sight of simple passersby,
but easy to find by those who know the rules,
today's speakeasies are very much back in vogue.

EMPLOYEES ONLY

The Employees Only cocktail bar opened in 2004, in the heart of Greenwich Village on the island of Manhattan, one of the most populated in the world. It was a project conceived by five friends with very different backgrounds, but with very similar visions for what would become their cocktail bar; a place that was convivial and elegant, but not flashy and where, above all, customers could find excellent cocktails, created with care using only the best ingredients. The Employees Only is this and a lot more. It is brightly lit with an array of paintings on the walls and a huge mirror that makes it even brighter. The wooden stools at the bar are rarely vacant, but there is a back dining room where dinner is served by reservation only; the food at Employees Only is definitely one of their strong suits. But the cocktails prepared by the bar's able bartenders are the main event, and whether you generally prefer one of the classics or a re-interpretation, we recommend that you try their version of the Manhattan. Hidden behind a fortune teller's storefront with a neon "Psychic" sign, it is not immediately clear that it is a cocktail bar. The atmosphere is pleasantly vintage, from the bartenders' uniforms to the old liquor bottles that fill the shelves, and the clientele is diversified. Connoisseurs come looking for the perfect cocktail, food lovers come for the kitchen's special dishes, and celebrity hunters come hoping to run into one of the bar's owners, Piper Perabo who played Violet in "Coyote Ugly". But whatever the category or the demand, Employees Only meets every expectation.

Keep in mind that on Sundays, the bar often offers burlesque shows and can get very crowded.

510 Hudson Street, New York City, USA
Telephone: +12122423021
employeesonlynyc.com

Lazy Lover

Avuá Prata Cachaça
Jalapeño infused Green Chartreuse
Bénédictine
Lime juice
Agave nectar

PDT

New York is considered the Speakeasy capital of the world, and PDT is probably the most sought-after secret bar in the city with potential clients vying for a tranquil spot to sit and sip a Paddington, one of the bar's most famous cocktails. The PDT (which stands for Please Don't Tell) has been serving cocktails in the East Village since May, 2007.

It is not difficult to find. Its address is well known and so is the name of the traditional American hot dog restaurant it hides behind, Crif Dogs, where exceptional hot dogs and beers are served. Once inside, you will see an old telephone booth that sits at the bottom of a few steps. Pick up the receiver. The only call the phone makes is to the PDT staff who will open the back wall of the booth and usher you into this "promised land" of mixed drinks. That is, of course, if you have made a reservation. PDT is extremely successful, so unless you have reserved ahead of time, you can either forget getting in or settle for a hot dog at Crif's.

Once inside, you will discover that the place is full of atmosphere. The decor is purposely minimalist. On one hand, it conveys the idea of the transitory nature of the place and on the other it keeps the focus on what the talented bartenders are making, whether it be the most classic of cocktails or a house specialty. The bar, with its bottles on display, is strikingly beautiful. There is an assortment of taxidermy animals, the most photographed of which is a grizzly bear with a hat that everyone calls Paddington. The seats are in leather, the sofas are classic Chesterfield, and the walls are exposed brick. It is certainly worth a visit, but remember not to brag about it too much afterwards. Like the name says, "Please Don't Tell".

113 St. Marks Place, New York City, USA
Telephone: +12126140386
pdtnyc.com

Paddington

1/4 oz Absinthe
1.5 oz White Rum
1/2 oz Lillet Blanc
1/2 oz Grapefruit juice
1/2 oz Lemon juice
1 tbsp Orange marmalade
Grapefruit twist for garnish

• Pour or spray the absinthe into a chilled glass. Swirl and tip the glass to fully coat its inner surface with the spirit. Pour out the absinthe and set the glass aside.
• Add the remaining ingredients to a cocktail shaker filled with ice.
• Shake, then strain into the absinthe-coated glass.
• Garnish with the grapefruit twist.

Please pick up phone reciever.

Press buzzer for 1-2 seconds.

Stay on phone, wait for instructions.

DO NOT buzz repeatedly.

Thank you.

RAINES LAW ROOM

This speakeasy in the heart of Chelsea was named after a New York State law issued in 1896 whose purpose it was to make life difficult for those who sold liquor and, consequently, for those who drank it. Simply put, the law said that no alcohol could be served on Sundays, except in hotels. Most workers' only day off was Sunday, so the ban heavily penalized bars, pubs and night clubs. But it did not take long for proprietors to come up with a countermeasure. They added small, sometimes fake rooms to their establishments and applied for a hotel license to get around the ban.

Today's Raines Law Room has all of the appeal of the secret bars of the 1920s with its vintage decor. Many of the pieces are original, including the splendid Chesterfield sofas.

Once inside, time seems to suddenly slow down, which is a fascinating contrast to the city outside

where everything always seems to go rushing by. There is plenty of time to decide what to drink and no pressure to call the waiter and order before you are ready—a good thing, especially on your first visit, since the cocktail list is long and exciting. It ranges from the great international classics of mixology to the most creative original recipes invented by an expert team of bartenders. When customers have decided what they want, they press a wall buzzer to call the waiter, just one more touch of vintage in a place where time seems to have stopped.

The Raines Law Room was inaugurated in 2005, and a second location was opened in 2014 at The William, a hotel in Midtown Manhattan. Maybe they were afraid that the Raines Law would go back into effect.

*Many modern speakeasies offer
an intentionally vintage atmosphere;
a veritable oasis that is perfect
for relaxing at the end of a long day.*

DEAR IRVING

It is hard to think of the Dear Irving as a single venue. The bar, opened in 2014 near Union Square, has five rooms that make it seem like four different bars. The outside of the bar is intentionally non-descript but once you are inside, you can choose from specific historical eras to time travel through spaces that evoke Marie Antoinette's France; Gertrude Stein, the American who inspired Ernest Hemingway's "Lost Generation" in his Paris years; President John F. Kennedy's America of the 1960s; the Roaring Twenties in the Great Gatsby-style room with partitioned compartments that lend an air of privacy; or the era of Abraham Lincoln, which is where you will find the bartenders at work behind the long bar. An evening at the Dear Irving is unforgettable and offers a variety of sensations according to where you choose to sit.

55 Irving Place, New York City, USA
dearirving.com

Every table has a buzzer to ring when you are ready to call the wait staff and order. Patrons seated at the bar can order directly from the bartenders and watch the performance as they work their magic with elegance and quick, measured movements, creating the tastes that linger briefly on the bar in tumblers and cocktail glasses. The atmosphere, the ambiance and the hospitality are all outstanding, and the same can be said for the drinks that the staff invites you to sip slowly and enjoy to the fullest. There are only a few rules at the Dear Irving, the ones we most strongly suggest are to reserve far enough in advance and then leave the adrenaline-charged atmosphere of the city and the tensions of daily life behind you, at least for a few hours.

I love Negroni #4

3/4 oz Gin
3/4 oz Sweet Vermouth
1/2 oz Aperol
1/2 oz St Germain
Rose petal infusion

• Stir.
• Serve in an Old Fashioned glass.

LE 4e MUR

You will find Le 4e Mur's address written at the bottom of this page, and while it may be enough to get you to the entrance, it will not be enough to get you through the door. The only option is to contact the bar and wait for a reply. As we know, speakeasies have rules that must be respected; after all, it is part of their appeal and this one in Montreal is no exception. But once you manage to gain access, you will discover a venue that revolves around the bar and the bartenders who shake, stir and pour a variety of cocktails made with flair and precision. The atmosphere is friendly and for the sake of courtesy, you will be asked to take off your hat when a woman is present.

Le 4e Mur opened in July, 2015 and soon found itself center stage in Montreal's nightlife. Once you have found the entrance, do not be fooled by the sign on the door that seems to indicate a private detective agency. Inside, a stairway leads to a warm, rustic room with lots of wood, rough stone walls, a few bookcases, comfortable leather arm chairs and a small stage where jazz and swing bands play. On Tuesdays and Saturdays, the climate heats up with burlesque shows. The venue is primarily a place to meet your friends in an intimate, softly-lit setting and sip a few cocktails in peace. There is also a covered, heated patio that patrons can enjoy all year, even in Canada's rigid winters, in French Bistro-style. There is never a risk of overcrowding since the bar's policy is not to admit more customers than there are seats for.

2021 St. Denis Street, Montreal, Canada
le4emur.com

The Riviera

London Dry gin
Campari
Luxardo Maraschino liqueur
Fresh pineapple
Lime juice, sugar and egg white

THE VIOLET HOUR

Chicago was, without a doubt, one of the busiest hubs for illegal liquor trafficking during Prohibition. It was headquarters for the most famous crime boss of the day, Al Capone, and its location on shores of Lake Michigan made it the perfect waterway to run bootleg liquor to the United States from Canada.

Even without the gangsters or illegal alcohol of the past, the Violet Hour manages to recreate the atmosphere of those dangerously fascinating times. Its interior is elegant and sophisticated, with blue leather high-back armchairs, small white candle-lit tables, a long marble bar, crystal chandeliers and a fireplace. The abundance of space and light is surprising and the heavy velvet drapes add a Great Gatsby-style vintage touch. Outside, there is no sign; just a bulb above the door marking the entrance. The façade features an ever-changing mural, and many visitors come expressly to admire the artwork created by a variety of international artists. The bar is acclaimed as a touchstone for cocktails in the city. Its name comes from a verse of T. S. Eliot's poem, "The Waste Land". Clients are selected and arranged so that everyone gets a seat. The house rules must be followed—appropriate attire, no baseball caps and no cell phones. And, as the last rule affably states, "Please do not bring anyone to the Violet Hour that you would not bring to your mother's house for Sunday dinner". Other than that, enjoy the atmosphere, pretend to be Di Caprio when he was still happy to be Gatsby, not at the end of the movie, and sit back and sip one of the many perfect cocktails the bar's talented bartenders will create for you.

1520 N. Damen Avenue, Chicago, Illinois, USA
Telephone: +17732521500
theviolethour.com

WILLIAMS & GRAHAM

The secret is kept on a shelf in the miniscule Williams & Graham bookstore. It is in a copy of Harry Craddock's "Savoy Cocktail Book", one of the bibles of bartenders throughout the world. Pull it out just a bit and the book case turns magically into the entrance to the real Williams & Graham, which is definitely not a bookstore. Customers fortunate enough to get in are greeted by the subtle, slightly nostalgic strains of the Mississippi Delta blues. The atmosphere is relaxed and unpretentious, modern but with an old-fashioned vibe. The imposing bar and bottle shelves are crammed beyond belief with every imaginable kind of liquor and spirits. The bartenders here are some of the best known in the United States, and their take on mixology is commendable. Their recipes are well grounded and perfectly dosed and they rarely contain more than 5 ingredients. Aromas and flavors leave an impression in an environment that exudes friendliness. The proprietors pride themselves on the "neighborhood bar" feeling that they have created, an atmosphere inspired by the bars their fathers and grandfathers knew where time seemed to stand still and the world was left outside the door. The excellent service is a mixture of formality and friendliness that keeps its customers coming back. The details are noteworthy; the 100-year-old tin ceiling, the bar and the display case behind it with its arched wooden niches, the Art Deco absinthe "fountain" and the table lamps with their subtle light. To put it simply, it is the ideal place to take a break from the quick pace of a routine work day; to share a conversation with the customers around you knowing that if they have come to Williams & Graham for a memorable evening, they appreciate the good life as much as you do.

3160 Tejon Street, Denver, Colorado, USA
Telephone: +13039978886
williamsandgraham.com

WILLIAMS & GRAHAM

Herbs, spices and homemade mixes.
In speakeasies, the cocktail culture thrives
with the revival of the great classics,
but also leaves room for new tendencies.

CIRCA 33

Speakeasies may no longer need to hide from the indiscreet eyes of the law, but one of the last places you would expect to find one is inside a cocktail bar. And yet, in Portland that is exactly where you will find this "secret" bar-within-a-bar.

The Circa 33 has an evocative atmosphere where Prohibition-themed events and the many classic cocktails proposed by the able bartenders make it feel like the Roaring Twenties. One of the many interesting details of the bar is that the cocktail menu is dated according to the year the drinks originated so customers can take a journey through history, maybe starting with a Hot Buttered rum, invented in 1862, moving on to a Tequila Gimlet (1928), then sipping a Moscow Mule (1941), and topping it off with a Michelada (1950). Obviously the menu also offers more recent concoctions; the re-interpretation of the classics as well as the latest expressions of the talent and creativity of Circa 33's bartenders.

All of this takes place inside the bar that everyone knows and can see from the outside, but only a privileged few know that the Circa 33 hides a secret space in what once was a pantry behind the kitchen. The entrance is hidden behind a bookcase, and getting in requires a few steps: first you have to move the book that hides the keypad where you must punch in the four-digit code that opens the door. But only a bartender can tell you the precise book and code. If you get in, though, you will be rewarded with an exclusive room furnished with leather armchairs, a shuffleboard table, and an old piano. But nothing should surprise you—not even the sight of the cook passing through with a crate of salad while you are sipping your drink. After all, it is a speakeasy, right?

CIRCA 33

BOURBON & BRANCH

The history of Bourbon & Branch is long and fascinating. From 1921 to 1933 a speakeasy operated illegally at this location behind the guise of "JJ Russell's Cigar Shop". John J. Russell was an industrious entrepreneur with connections to the most notorious bootleggers, and since the location had been a bar prior to the Volstead Act, Russell had only to change the sign outside and continue to satisfy what was already a solid base of loyal customers. He did not sell many cigars, but the speakeasy managed to stay out of the sights of the Prohibition agents and was never raided.

In order to gain access to Bourbon & Branch today, you must follow a few fundamental rules: speak in hushed tones (obviously), do not use a cell phone, do not remain standing, do not take photos and, above all, do not even think about ordering a Cosmopolitan. The atmosphere is a suggestive mixture of well-worn elements; from the wooden floor with its air of vintage luxury to the chandelier that hangs from the ceiling like a wildflower. The walls are mostly of exposed brick, and behind the bar, niches in the bricks hold endless bottles of premium liquors and spirits including a sensational selection of bourbons. Inside the main bar is the entrance to the secret room known as "The Library", which is only accessible to those who know the password. Apparently, the "emergency exits" are still functional—five secret underground tunnels that may not be necessary today, but that were fundamental escape routes during the days of Prohibition. All of the qualities of an excellent bartender shine when you taste one of the bar's perfectly balanced cocktails. But in order to do so, you first have to find the entrance—an unmarked door with a spyhole and a buzzer. We will give you a hint: look for the Anti-Saloon League sign. The irony is indisputable.

501 Jones Street, San Francisco, California, USA
Telephone: +14153461735
bourbonandbranch.com

BOURBON & BRANCH

THE LAUNDRY ROOM

At first glance, the outside of the Laundry Room looks a little like Edward Hopper's famous painting "Nighthawks". It sits on a corner with big pane windows that light up the night and a neon sign that can be confusing. The sign says "Commonwealth" and belongs to a cocktail bar that is popular with tourists and locals, in what is the most famous city in Nevada and one of the most famous in the world. Known as the "City of Lights" or "Sin City", it has been depicted in dozens of movies and television series. The Commonwealth is a stylish bar with a captivating atmosphere, excellent cocktails and a great selection of beers. But the Commonwealth has a secret within its walls; a secret that will only be revealed when the right door opens. In true speakeasy tradition, the door is anonymous and can be easily overlooked. It only opens for those who have sent a text to a secret number for instructions on how to enter. Getting the number is not easy, but once you are in, you will discover the Commonwealth's secret—The Laundry Room, the bar within a bar. This backroom bar is welcoming but can accommodate only 20 customers at a time, the same as the number of cocktails on the menu every evening.

The Laundry Room opened in 2012 when its "host", the Commonwealth opened. It soon became one of the best places in the city for a perfectly crafted cocktail. The ambiance is refined but friendly, and the rules prohibit cell phones, photos and unnecessary noise. Conversations are held in the hushed tones of the speakeasies of the 1920s. Outside, the Las Vegas Strip is a vortex of lights and sounds, enormous hotels and casinos and of crowds hailing from every corner of the world. Anyone who comes here knows there is no escaping the excitement of the city, but knowing that in the middle of it all there is an oasis like the Laundry Room is reassuring, to say the least.

525 Fremont Street, Las Vegas, Nevada, USA
Telephone: +17027011466

Berried in Sin

1 oz Cassis

1 oz London Dry gin

1 oz Lime

1/4 oz Simple syrup

1/2 oz Egg white

• Shake all of the ingredients together and pour into a glass over 3/4 of an ounce of Champagne.

• Garnish with crushed mint leaves and 5 drops of Angostura bitters.

CELEBRATING

TOWNHOUSE
1915-2015
VENICE

100 YEARS

· December 5TH 2015 ·

THE DEL MONTE SPEAKEASY

On the vast and growing horizon of modern speakeasies, The Del Monte is a legend. It was a true speakeasy that lived a colorful existence during Prohibition. In 1915 an Italian immigrant, Cesare Menotti, opened the Townhouse Bar in Venice Beach, the legendary Los Angeles location immortalized in an endless array of movies and television series and frequented by cult figures like Jim Morrison.

The bar was successful and attracted a substantial group of regular patrons until the enactment of Prohibition in January, 1920 when, along with many other establishments of the era, it seemed destined to close. But Menotti did not lose heart. He turned the Townhouse into a grocery store as a cover, but under the crates of produce was a basement that could only be accessed through a trap door. That basement was the Del Monte. Far from prying eyes, the liquor continued to flow, and today the Del Monte is one of the oldest bars in the Los Angeles area.

It is a fascinating space that has maintained all of its original charm. Simple basement-style pillars support a low ceiling, but the bar that runs almost the entire length of the wall is a true eye-catcher. You can sit on one of the round stools and watch the bartenders ply their craft, or you can have a seat on the long leather sofa or at one of the cocktail tables. The Del Monte often features entertainment, including live music, DJs, comedy and burlesque. But above all it features cocktails—the great classics and the newly created—to drink in the bracing atmosphere of when doing so was illegal and defiant.

52 Windward Avenue, Venice, Los Angeles, California, USA
Telephone: +13103924040
townhousevenice.com

Old Fashioned

Buffalo Trace Bourbon
Knob Creek Rye
Demerara Syrup
Angostura Bitters

*Some establishments, like the Del Monte
in Los Angeles, came through the era
of Prohibition unscathed and are, even now,
a point of reference for true connoisseurs.*

777 G Street, San Diego, California, USA
Telephone: +16198884713
nobleexperimentsd.com

NOBLE EXPERIMENT

It was President Herbert Hoover who defined Prohibition as a "great social and economic experiment, noble in motive . . ." and that definition gave its name to a bar that is secretly located in a popular restaurant in downtown San Diego. What looks like a small stack of beer kegs is actually the entrance to the Noble Experiment, a splendid bar with an unusual but tastefully balanced decor. Rembrandt-style paintings and a crystal chandelier counterbalance an entire wall covered with nestled bronze skulls, perhaps slightly disturbing, but which is also undeniably charming. More important, the outstanding bartenders demonstrate their creativity and technique in each of the seven hundred kinds of cocktails they create, mixing over a hundred types of liquors with homemade syrups, fruit and fruit juices.

The Noble Experiment opened its doors in 2010 and soon became a success, both locally and beyond. In fact, in order to get in, customers need to reserve at least a week in advance. Instructions about how to reserve are on the bar's website; the only information you will find there because the establishment likes to be discreet—no overly-casual attire, no flip-flops or baseball caps, and no flash photos. If you have powered your way through the endless list of cocktails and you still do not know what to order, just explain your tastes to the bartender and wait to savor the result. Which, according to the most inveterate patrons, will be anything but disappointing.

Old Timber

2 oz Stagg Jr. Barrel
 Strenght Bourbon
1/4 oz Averna
1/4 oz El Dorado Falernum
2 dashes of orange bitters
 Smith & Cross Jamaican
 Rum

• Mix the ingredients for a few seconds in an Old Fashioned
glass with ice.
• Top it off with the Jamaican Rum and garnish with
mint sprigs.

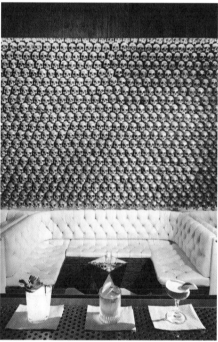

JULES BASEMENT

One of Mexico City's beautiful tree-lined boulevards is the first thing you see on your way to Jules Basement. It conveys the feeling of both the serenity and the dynamism of a big city. The second thing you see is a bit different. A white, anonymous refrigerator door that resembles the one on the walk-in freezer where Wendy Torrance locks up her husband Jack in one of the most renowned scenes in Stanley Kubrick's masterpiece, "The Shining." But have no fear, this is not the Overlook Hotel, and there is no frozen food behind that door. In reality, it opens onto an exquisite, captivating bar that features live music almost every night and where excellent cocktails are served in a friendly atmosphere.

If and when you get in (reservations are strongly suggested), follow the steps down to the bar. You will find a modern, elegant, plain white space, somehow reminiscent of the refrigerator door, where great attention has been paid to detail. Patrons can sit around cube-shaped, glass tables with white Damien Hirst-style skulls encased within, or at the two-sided bar where they have a better view of the bartenders as they ply their trade. Working with a seemingly infinite selection of spirits and liquors; aguardiente, whiskey, and obviously the nationally beloved tequila and mezcal, the bartenders will astonish both your eyes and your palate. All of their re-interpretations of the classics are noteworthy. Particular interesting is their Negroni made with mezcal, their Guatemala Sazerac with rum in place of rye whiskey or cognac, and their enigmatic Flor de Sangre made with tequila, hibiscus flower, agave nectar and fresh lime.

93 Calle Julio Verne, Polanco, Mexico City, Mexico
Telephone: +525552801278
julesbasement.com

Precision, dexterity and a profound knowledge of the vast array of ingredients. The barman always plays a fundamental role in the fascination of a speakeasy. The person behind the bar is the star of the show.

EAU DE VIE

Eau de Vie translated to "aqua vitae" or the water of life, was the name Latins gave to all alcoholic beverages. Spirits were considered deeply significant and strongly connected to health and longevity, perhaps because at the time, drinking alcohol was often less of a health risk than drinking water. The term was mystical and archaic, but there is nothing archaic about this half-hidden cocktail bar behind the Kirketon Hotel, even if its atmosphere and plush vintage decor give a bit of a nod to the Roaring Twenties and Prohibition. A seat at one of the comfortable stools at the bar affords a view of the over five hundred different labels the expert bartenders use to work their magic, as well as the chance to chat with them while they work. There is a table to accommodate groups, a number of smaller tables for couples, and a long leather sofa that borders three of the bar's walls. A pinch of humor is added to the precision and meticulousness that go into the cocktails; watching the bartenders work with a shaker shaped like a woman's leg is proof and so is their Banderillero cocktail, a mix of chorizo-flavored mezcal, pineapple vinegar, Aperol, lime and Habanero bitter served in a real bull's horn. But there is more. A secret door leads to the Whisky Room—a speakeasy-within-a-speakeasy—where patrons can relax with one of the hundreds of whiskies selected by the staff. The Whisky Room has private bottle-lockers for the more fortunate guests as well as an exclusive range of rare and hard to find spirits. Eau de Vie also hosts masterclasses, where expert bartenders give patrons the opportunity to learn the history and preparation techniques of each single cocktail and possibly become experts in their own right, capable of crafting perfect cocktails at home. Eau de Vie is not just a place to drink, it is a place to learn how to drink.

229 Darlinghurst Road, Sydney, Australia
Telephone: +610422263226
eaudevie.com.au

Modern speakeasies seem to have legitimized all of the most refined and innovative techniques, and the result is an array of new sensations for today's patrons.

BAR NAYUTA

The Nayuta calls itself a "nocturnal pharmacy" and as a matter of fact, the shelves behind the bar are lined not just with liquor bottles, but also with jars of herbs and spices that the knowledgeable bartenders use in their concoctions. Located in the area of Triangle Park, one of the busiest squares in downtown Osaka, the bar is hidden from the view of the unwitting passerby. But Osaka's cocktail connoisseurs know where to find it; as the bar's owners say: "All you need is enough motivation." A helpful hint is to look for an esoteric sign painted on a brick wall, but if that should fail, you can always call the bar's phone number and as they promise on their website: "We are gonna go get you!". The signature house cocktails are the result of great passion and with extensively studied ingredients, the bartenders concoct an array of particular sensations that surprise even the most experienced palates. Homemade bitters, infusions and gin give a unique touch to even the best-known classic cocktails. The decor is magnificent with its majestic curved bar dominating the room. The bar regularly accommodates both locals and visitors who are seeking authenticity and class, and even though the drink preparation is meticulously professional, the ambiance is informal and friendly. In other words, the ideal place to relax and meet people with, of course, your cocktail glass in hand.

Nishishinsaibashi, Chuo-ku, Osaka, Japan
Telephone: +810662103615
bar-nayuta.com

Rain Drop

1.5 oz Bay leaf
 infused Gin
1/2 oz Homemade
 compound gin
2/3 oz Fresh lime juice
2/3 oz Simple syrup
Cucumber cubes, a pinch
 of salt, dried bay leaf, a
 pinch of dried lavender,
 cherry wood chips for
 smoking.

• Mix all ingredients except the dried herbs.
• Light the wood chips and capture the smoke in another container.
• Shake the ingredients with the smoke and abundant ice. Double strain into a Nick & Nora glass.
• Heat the dried bay leaf without burning it and place it on the glass.
• Add a pinch of lavender and serve.

From the United States to the Far East
and from Europe to Australia, the speakeasy
phenomenon has become an international trend
that knows no bounds.

OUNCE

A group of friends grew up in the shadows of Manhattan skyscrapers often drinking a cocktail of the same name in a city considered the capital of drinks with a particular dedication to the concept of speakeasies. These friends had an idea upon their return to Taipei: the Ounce cocktail bar; a place that would propose the great classics of mixology in an elegant but informal context. The idea became reality in 2012. Today, the Ounce is in every guide to Taiwan. It is easy to find if you know what to look for and you are not fooled by first impressions.

In fact, there is a coffee house at the address with a sign that says "Relax - The Espresso Place", which happens to serve a great cup of coffee if that is what you want. But if it is one of the best cocktails in the city that you are looking for, you will have to look a little closer to find the secret door and ring the doorbell to get in. Inside, the decor is minimal but memorable. The focus is entirely on two things: the cocktails and the informal, friendly atmosphere. The first requires unfailing attention to the no-nonsense aromas and flavors that fill the customers' glasses, and the second is based on the personalities of Ounce's bartenders and patrons. The bar is a favorite of locals and a success with a lot of business travelers and tourists, offering a selection of liquors and spirits that no other establishment in the city can vaunt. The atmosphere is friendly and relaxed, even if it gets decidedly livelier on the weekend.

309 Section 4, Xinyi Road, Da'an District, Taipei, Taiwan
Telephone: +886227037761
ouncetaipei.com

001

During the day, the neighborhood vibrates with the noise and the people who crowd the streets of the market; buyers and sellers and dozens of stalls. But in the evening, after hours, the din of the crowds subsides, and what is left is one of the most glamorous bars in Hong Kong. It is easy to miss since it is hidden behind a row of shuttered stalls and its unmarked black door has only a brass doorbell to identify it. But once you are inside, the magic begins. The decor is sophisticated with strategically placed Art Deco-styled ceiling lamps, aqua-green leather armchairs and booths and an elegant bar. 001's intuitive bartenders interpret the tastes of their patrons and go above and beyond the frequently changing drink menu of about twenty cocktails. Just strike up a conversation and your satisfaction is guaranteed. A menu of superior snacks and shareable plates gives customers the sustenance they need to be able to have one more cocktail. The soft classical jazz that flows through the speakers accompanies the conversation and gives the bar the air of an exclusive club, light years away from the rowdy, frenetic atmosphere of Hong Kong's center. The 001 is very popular with locals and tourists alike. It calls itself a modern speakeasy and without overly indulging in 1920s nostalgia, it projects the same mysterious air. Considering the bar's strictly respected no-standing policy, reservations well in advance are strongly suggested.

97 Wellington Street, Hong Kong, China
Telephone: +85228106969

6 Duddell Street, Central, Hong Kong, China
Telephone: +85221168949
foxglovehk.com

FOXGLOVE

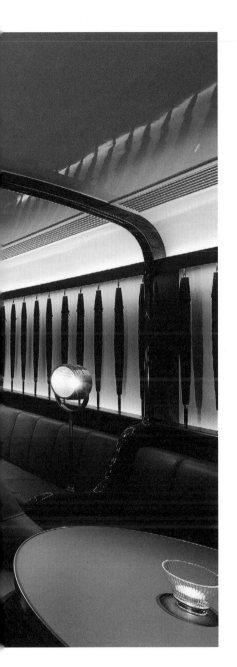

It is difficult to say whether the name of this renowned establishment in Hong Kong was inspired by the simple beauty of the digitalis flower or by its duplicitous and ambiguous nature: therapeutic in controlled doses and potentially fatal when taken in excess. In either case, its name certainly adds to the somewhat mysterious charm of the Foxglove. At face value, fortunate visitors will find an elegant umbrella shop, meticulously outfitted with silver-handled umbrellas displayed as collectors' items in a vault. But walk through the alcove and press down on a "certain" umbrella, and you will find yourself in an atmosphere of bygone opulence that feels like a 1950s luxury liner or maybe a space ship of the period. Clean lines and contrasting colors together with the long, very well-stocked bar give a sense of order, logic and rationality. One travel-themed room is reminiscent of a vintage first-class train compartment and in another, movie buffs relax in what could be the cabin of the Zeppelin that Indiana Jones and his father used to try to escape from the Germans in "Indiana Jones and the Last Crusade." The bar's elegance and refinement are immediately appreciable, as is the quality of the cocktails it serves; great timeless classics with an innovative twist. The food at the Foxglove is also a focal point. High profile cuisine combines raw materials and techniques from a variety of nations—in other words, the kitchen of a true traveler. Their prestigious liquor collection includes, among other things, distilled spirits, cognac, brandy and Japanese whiskey, some of which date back to the 1930s or to distilleries that closed long ago. From Tuesday to Saturday, the bar features live entertainment with a certain preference for jazz that, on occasions, makes room for blues, soul and pop.

FOXGLOVE

93/95 Ground Floor, Seil Kan Thar Road (Lower Block) Kyauttadar, Yangon, Myanmar
Telephone: +959786833847
blindtiger-yangon.com

THE BLIND TIGER

During Prohibition, whispering in speakeasies was not a question of
courtesy but a necessity. Hushed voices made it more difficult for the police
to identify the bars that served illegal liquor. The Blind Tiger was a real
speakeasy when it opened in 2015. In Myanmar it was a moment of political
transition from a military regime to a democratic government; a period
in which it was legal to drink alcohol, but in which expressing political or
religious opinions could land you in jail. The Blind Tiger was one of the few
places where patrons could freely discuss any subject, as long as they did
it in a whisper. Today, the climate in Myanmar is decidedly more relaxed,
and although the bar's location on a busy street in downtown Yangon is no
secret, the Blind Tiger is still hard to find. Look around you and try to spot the
tiger's claw—it is the only indication that you have arrived at your destination.

A sensor in front of the door lets the staff know you are there. Once they
have taken a look at you through the spyhole and you have been approved,
you will be ushered into an establishment that is both elegant and discreet.
Its sumptuous lounge has exposed brick walls that are lined with tables and
leather armchairs on one side and a long bar on the other. The cutting-edge
art of local painters that is regularly displayed attracts a variety of patrons,
but the bartenders are the true artists here; mixing up refined cocktails that
include the great international classics and a range of original signature
drinks. A favorite is always the Pegu Club cocktail, born here in Myanmar in
the bar of the same name. The bar opened in 1882 to serve visiting British
officers and gentlemen and quickly became one of the most famous haunts
in Southeast Asia. But the Pegu Club no longer exists and the coolest place
to be in Myanmar today is the Blind Tiger, where you will find a cosmopolitan
mix of discerning locals and curious visitors.

*"I feel sorry for people that don't drink,
because when they wake up in the morning,
that's as good as they're going to feel all day."*
Frank Sinatra

THE SPEAKEASY

It is just a few hundred meters from Syntagma Square, the seat of the Greek Parliament, but it only takes a minute to get lost in the alleyways of Athens' historical center. A better option is to reach the bar virtually, through its Facebook page; that way you will be assured of both the address and a reservation which you most definitely need to get into this small, but recently expanded, underground venue, especially on the weekend. The Speakeasy has a rather complicated history. It was originally conceived as a "normal" bar known for its jazz music soirees in a suburb north of Athens. In 2013, when it moved to the city center, it decided to make itself inconspicuous to passersby and become what its name promised. Today, you only need to go down the steps to find yourself in the exclusive, if not mysterious, atmosphere

that characterized the speakeasies of the Prohibition era. It is more the sense of transiency than the furnishings that create the ambiance in the Speakeasy, that feeling of belonging to an elite few that have found a place all their own. It does not take long for patrons to begin socializing among themselves while they watch the skilled bartenders use their talents to create a selection of perfectly balanced cocktails. The drink menu of about twenty cocktails changes more or less on a yearly basis and includes original creations, many of which are made with homemade syrups, infusions, and traditional Greek spirits such as Mastiha. But the fundamentals of the profession are manifest at the Speakeasy, and the Old Fashioned you can get here is the proof.

Bitter Harvest

Rye Whiskey

Averna liqueur

Pimento infused rum

• Mix with ice and serve in a tumbler.

2 Via Vannella Gaetani, Naples, Italy
Telephone: +390817645390

L'ANTIQUARIO

There was a time when this street in the center of Naples, a stone's throw from the most famous gulf in Italy, was known for its antique shops. And in fact, a shop is exactly what to look for here, but one with a very particular back room. L'Antiquario, disguised as an antique shop, is actually a secret bar; but there is no need for a password to get in, just reserve in advance and knock on the door. What you will find is an enclave of quality drinking in a quiet atmosphere far from the traffic of the city. The ambiance is elegantly intimate with soft lights, red velvet sofas and vintage novelties here and there; a distinct 1920s speakeasy style. But the bar's cocktails span a much wider time frame. They are divided into three categories; classic, such as the Mai Tai and the St. Regis Mint Julep; contemporary, like the Cosmopolitan and the Moscow Mule; and modern, meaning cocktails that have broken with tradition and are characteristically innovative and avant-garde. Every drink is presented with its pedigree and a reference to its culture and history.

For lovers of "bubbly", the Champagne selection is exceptional. The same can be said of the food menu, which ranges from smoked salmon to Iberian prosciutto, and from anchovies of the Cantabrian Sea to caviar.

Recognized as a cocktail bar of absolute excellence in Italy, L'Antiquario is managed by one of its owners, Alexander Frezza, one of the best-known names in the business.

Mulata Daiquiri

2 oz Gold cuban rum
2/3 oz Dark cocoa liqueur
1/3 oz Sugar syrup
1 oz Lime juice

• Unsweetened cocoa powder to rim the glass.

30 Vicolo Cellini, Rome, Italy
Telephone: +390696845937
thejerrythomasproject.it

JERRY THOMAS PROJECT

The Jerry Thomas Project is named after an extremely famous barman of the 19th century. Widely considered the progenitor of American mixology, he is the author of "The Bartender's Guide", which is still one of the bibles of the profession. The venue, opened in 2009 in Rome, is a forerunner as one of the first speakeasy style bars in Italy. Its work approach behind the bar is innovative as well; research to uncover the earliest recipes for classic cocktails entails a "purging" process that eliminates the innumerable modifications made by successive generations of barmen. Only then can the cocktails be presented in their original versions, albeit sometimes with a creative twist. Behind the bar's undisputed success is research and dedication that is not limited just to mixology; other subjects considered marginal to the art of mixing—herbal medicine, for example—are cultivated as well, as is a distinctive flair for telling a story, sometimes its own. And then, of course, there is the ambience. The entrance is in a dark, non-descript alley in the heart of Rome, near Piazza Navona and Campo de' Fiori. It has a spyhole that allows the door staff to ask the frequently changing password, which is the answer to a question hidden on the bar's website. Inside, there is a limited number of seats (just over thirty), the most sought after of which are the four stools at the bar. Live music adds to the mood a couple of nights a week, and is exclusively Roaring Twenties-type jazz. But what makes the difference is the mastery of the bartenders. The superb level of their bartending and mixology know-how give depth and intensity to every sip.

To make what is probably Jerry Thomas's most famous cocktail, the Blue Blazer, flaming whiskey was passed back and forth between two mixing glasses, creating a spectacular fiery arc.

Improved Aviation

Crocodile Gin del
 Professore
Quaglia violet liqueur
Lavander syrup
Lemon juice
Rosehip Bitters

• Shake and strain into a cocktail glass.
• Garnish with a lemon twist.

MALKOVICH

One of Winston Churchill's famous lines, "It's a riddle, wrapped in a mystery, inside an enigma" is an appropriate introduction to the Malkovich in Genoa, a highly secret venue that keeps its address under tight wraps. In order to have the pleasure of occupying a seat at the bar, or even one of the very limited seats within (around 40), you must call the number at the bottom of this page. No one will answer, but you will receive a text message with an address and business hours and a question, the answer to which will get you across the threshold. You will need to be versed in movie trivia to navigate this obstacle course; it is the leitmotif of the venue's password questions as well as its cocktail list.

Work on the project was underway for well over a year when the bar opened in 2015. There are three rooms besides the barroom and the ambiance throughout is intentionally 1930s with vintage bottles, glasses, and shakers. The walls are lined with pictures of famous directors and classic cinema posters, and the drinks evoke the hundreds of cocktails that were immortalized in countless movie hits. From the Voodoo Sazerac, a tribute to the New Orleans cocktail that was made famous in the James Bond movie "Live and Let Die" which was set there, to a recrafting of the White Russian that was a constant for the Dude in "The Big Lebowski".

Finding the Malkovich is not simple, but the skilled bartenders and the fascinating atmosphere make the effort worthwhile, as it is useful also to brush up on your movie trivia.

Genoa, Italy
Telephone: +393930110393
malkovich.it

MALKOVICH

Small works of art. Today's cocktails have to be more than "good", they also have to be "good-looking", but always in that order of importance.

MAD DOG SOCIAL CLUB

You can pass by dozens of times and still miss it; unless, of course, you have the address. You will recognize the place by the logo on its doorbell—a stylized black dog—then all you have to do is walk down a few steps into what might be just any basement. But of course it is not.

Instead, you will find yourself in a warm and inviting club that opened in 2014 with the idea of changing the "alcoholic" habits of people who frequent cocktail bars in Italy. So no spritzes, no mojitos; in their place, reclamation of classic mixology and its timeless cocktails, served under a veil of almost absolute secrecy. When it first opened, the only way to get into the Mad Dog was by word of mouth, in the company of a regular customer and, of course, after having made a reservation. Though the bar still has the air of a private club, it may be a bit easier to get in now, even if it is still invisible unless you know it is there. The bar is in the first room along with several 20-liter oak barrels that the owners use not to age vermouth, as was done traditionally in Turin, but rather to refine the taste of their cocktails for a period of six to nine months. As Charles Darwin knew, evolution can be surprising!

On the average, the clientele is relatively young, about 35, and enjoys the live music featured two nights a week. The music, often piano, is kept soft and low, a background for conversation with other customers and with Matteo Rubuffo's team of bartenders. No one wants to miss the tales that are hiding in a cocktail glass. What could be better?

35A Via Maria Vittoria, Turin, Italy
Telephone: +390118120874
themaddog.it

Mad Dog Negroni

1.3 oz London Dry Gin
1.25 oz Red Vermouth
 del Professore
1 oz Grapefruit and
 chamomile infused
 Campari
2/3 oz French Vermouth

• Stir & strain.
• Garnish with lemon and orange twists.

1930

You can pass in front of the display window with the waving golden Chinese cats dozens of times and still have absolutely no idea what is on the other side. There really is nothing that draws your attention, which is no surprise since the 1930 is the best-hidden venue under the Milanese sky. It is so secret that its address is not published, its website seems inoperative, and what little information is available takes potential patrons on something of a wild goose chase to other establishments owned by the 1930's proprietor. The pilgrimage is worth it, if for nothing other than the allure of an exclusive club. But there is much more—the basement with its vaulted ceiling in exposed brick, the ground floor with its air of a tastefully furnished period drawing room and, of course, the drinks. Here, cocktails are the expression of a provocative art and include the use of strange and sometimes obscure ingredients such as "distilled earth", algae infused gin, red rice syrup, distilled gorgonzola and anything else that might occur to Marco Russo, the bar's acrobatic owner, who can view customers as they enter without being seen.

The bar opened in 2013 and has become a point of reference in Milan. Its name, 1930, does not refer to a year, but to a street number, 19, and the number on the sign outside, 30. Regular customers can vaunt a personalized membership card with their name engraved, but bear in mind that there are a number of necessary steps to take before you are given one, the first of which is simply to get in.

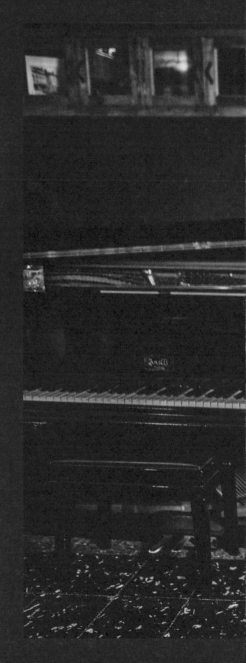

Milan, Italy
1930milano@gmail.com

Lighthouse of Scotland

1.5 oz Single Malt Scotch whiskey
1/4 oz Sea water
1/3 oz 1930 distilled earth
1.5 oz Vanilla Belhaven Beer syrup
1 dash of milk
8 drops Aromatic bitters

The Parlour Mule

1.3 oz Ketel One Vodka

1/2 oz Homemade spiced berry syrup

1/3 oz Fresh squeezed lime juice

3 dashes of Angostura Bitters

2/3 oz Homemade ginger syrup

1 oz Soda

• Serve in a glass.

• Garnish with a generous amount of berries, a mint sprig, some edible flowers and a sprinkle of gold colored dust.

THE PARLOUR

Near the Opera Theater in Frankfurt, The Parlour has been lighting up the night since 2012. But you would never know it from the outside. In keeping with the tradition of secret bars, its exterior gives no indication of what is on the inside and even the street it is located on is rather anonymous. But behind the door hides one of the most exclusive cocktail bars in the city. The clean, essential lines of its modern decor are enhanced with a beautiful Chesterfield sofa, in dark wood, a few stools at the bar and a vast number of tables and armchairs to relax in for an enjoyable evening among friends. Here, the art of the cocktail expresses itself in a kaleidoscope of colors. Herbs, flowers and other homemade touches contribute to making cocktails that are a delight even just to behold. But to stop at the aesthetics would be a pity since your other senses would miss the stimulating fragrances and tastes. It is worth your while to take a moment to admire the originality of the garnish or of the stemware that goes far beyond the classic tumblers or Martini glasses, but the true excellence of The Parlour is found in the perfect harmony of their ingredients, and in the smooth or sometimes penetrating energy of their cocktails. The bartenders are perfectly adept at preparing great cocktail classics, but are at their best when given free rein to conjure up drinks of their own inspiration. The clientele is elegant and international and the music is always enjoyable. The bar can get crowded on the weekends, but it is always worth a try to get in.

6 Zwingergasse, Frankfurt, Germany
theparlour.de

La Jana

1.3 oz Tanqueray Gin
2/3 oz Fresh lemon juice
2/3 oz St. Germain
2/3 oz White Lillet
Mint
5 White grapes

• Shake with ice.
• Serve in a Martini glass.

DIE ROTE BAR

Gentlemen serving other gentlemen. This beautiful, poignant vision sums up the fascination of the Rote Bar. The bar opened in 1995 in a building that has been home to public establishments that have sold alcohol for almost 200 years, since 1824 to be exact. It is no surprise that there is no sign outside. There never has been; you find the place if you know it or at least know the address. Finding the bar with its non-descript exterior is the price you have to pay to enjoy the vintage charm of the interior with its soft lights, table lamps, striking chandelier and a very original bar front panel that is punctuated by tiny lights. The atmosphere is that of an exclusive, albeit informal, club, inviting a diversified, international clientele all of whom love a good drink and good conversation with people from a variety of cultures. Red is the dominating color from the lights to the furnishings, but the white coats of the bar staff are a sign that here, the bartenders learn their profession in the traditional school, founded on precision and the simplicity of everlasting class. So there is little room here for the avant-garde mixology that sometimes risks becoming an end in itself; rather, here the emphasis is on well-implemented know-how and guaranteed satisfaction. There are few rules for guests (no shorts, undershirts, or beachwear in general for the men) except to demonstrate a respect for tradition and for each other. In other words, the respect of gentlemen among gentlemen in a traditional men's club where the rules need not be explained because they are ingrained in every member. The Rote Bar has everything it takes to be a point of reference in Frankfurt's nightlife. That is, of course, if you deserve it.

7 Mainkai, Frankfurt, Germany
rotebar.com

Soft lights, warm hues, a subtle atmosphere.
A lot of modern speakeasies have adopted
these characteristics as their "trademark".
Why? To make their clientele feel at home.

REINGOLD

The lavishly decorated Reingold Bar is in Mitte, Berlin's most central neighborhood, across the Spree River from the famous Brandenburg Gate. The atmosphere is one of elegance with a long bar and low lighting. A series of mirrors and striking murals decorate the walls and the spectacular outdoor seating area is visible only once you get inside. But, from the outside, the entrance is a sharp contrast to the splendor of the "gilded" interior and the sign that says Reingold Bar is the only indication that this is a place to get something to drink. "Something" is, of course, too generic a word for the quality of the cocktails, as well as for the flair and precision of the bar staff, and the sophisticated atmosphere of the Reingold stands out among a plethora of venues in a city that in recent years has become an international night-life destination. The bar features live DJ sets and bands playing a mix of jazz, swing and hip hop on the weekend and friendly, professional service all week long.

The drink list is extensive and includes a number of re-interpretations of the classics and many original signature drinks, but if you do not find what you want on the menu, ask the bartender to make a recommendation. You will not be disappointed.

The bar is spacious but maintains a warm, welcoming ambiance that can accommodate a crowd with plush armchairs and sofas throughout, and the long bar offers plentiful seating for patrons who like to sit face-to-face with the bartender. The result is that the bar is one of the busiest in the city, so before you take a fun-filled, satisfaction-guaranteed dive into Berlin's nightlife at the Reingold, we strongly suggest you make a reservation.

11 Novalisstrasse, Berlin, Germany
Telephone: +493028387676
cms.reingold.de

Hispanola Buccaneer

1 oz Clairin Sajous rum
1/2 oz Kaffeegeist (coffee liqueur)
1/4 oz Verjus
1/3 oz PX Sherry
dash of Bittermen`s Tiki Bitter

• Shake and serve over ice.
• Garnish with sprinklings of thyme leaves.

BECKETTS KOPF

The piercing gaze of the Nobel Prize winning author and playwright Samuel Beckett staring down at you as you study the cocktail list can be unnerving, but pay no attention. Instead, keep your interest focused on the bartender. His quick, precise, almost surgical moves, will reward you with an excellent cocktail. The atmosphere in Becketts Kopf is extremely relaxing and welcoming with dim lighting, comfortable leather armchairs, and a gorgeous front bar that we would all like to have at home. The cocktail list is a tribute to the spirit of Beckett and his works. Printed on what appear to be old copies of Beckett's plays, the most famous of which is probably "Waiting for Godot", the ample selection of drinks is intelligently divided into categories according to their most characteristic flavors and aromas. There is no need to be cocktail experts or memorize the drink menu; just let your fancy or palate be your guide and if you still have doubts, the knowledgeable bar staff will quell them with their professional expertise.

The bar, open since 2004, has a speakeasy air of privacy and tranquility that requires clients to respect a few rules, such as not entering if you have already had enough to drink elsewhere and not coming in large groups, given that the bar's capacity is limited to the number of seats provided. The care that goes into the selection of spirits and other ingredients borders on the maniacal. Because Becketts works closely with small producers and distillers, it is able to obtain, in most cases, careful control over production. Among its own craft products is its signature "Milano-style" digestive liqueur. Many of the cocktails hark back to before the Prohibition era, and all of them are served in vintage glassware. From the outside there is nothing to indicate the location of the Becketts Kopf except for a doorbell, but once you are in the neighborhood, look for the iconic face of the Irish playwright; he will show you the way.

64 Pappelallee, Berlin, Germany
becketts-kopf.de

Salty Peanut Old Fashioned

Peanut & Sea Salt Rum
Maple syrup
Bitters

DRIP BAR

One drop at a time. Because patience is the virtue of the strong, and because this is one of the characteristics that distinguishes this hard to recognize venue in Hamburg. A few indications beyond just the address are necessary. Once you are on the right street, look for a door that, at first glance, resembles a page filled by graffiti artists. The drapes on the windows that face the street are so dark and heavy that nothing filters out, but there is a doorbell near the door. And that is the bell to ring to get in.

On the other side of the threshold, the Drip Bar shows its true colors—a decidedly intimate and hospitable place. There are thirty-five seats and when they are full, no one else is admitted because the staff likes to keep the right atmosphere and to offer excellent service, another feature of the Drip Bar. The first, though, is the one we mentioned at the outset. The bar has revived a Japanese technique that requires time, but that also yields fascinating results. Behind the bar are what at first seem like enormous hour glasses, but that in reality are Cold Brew Drippers, ordinarily used to prepare a particular kind of coffee. The coffee goes in the middle section and the water that goes in the top passes through it "one drop at a time". The process, which usually takes about seven hours, can take up to seventy-two hours with these particular "hour glasses". Another important difference is that in these drippers, the water has been replaced with ten year old rum and peanuts seasoned with sea salt take the place of the coffee. The final result is a unique rum that will become the signature ingredient in the Salty Peanut Old Fashioned; as will the vodka, dripped through red beetroots, in the Beetroot Gimlet; and the gin, filtered through hibiscus flowers and mixed into the Last Word. It is a great sight to behold, to the accompaniment of background music, right down to the last drop.

4 Antonistrasse, Hamburg, Germany
dripbar.de

DOOR 74

Among the thousands of doors in Amsterdam, there is one secret
one that opens onto the first, historical speakeasy, not just of
Amsterdam, but of the Netherlands, and Luxembourg. Since it
opened in 2008, it has been a very well-kept secret from the hordes
of tourists that flock to the city every year. Obviously, if you have
the address, finding the place will be a little easier, but if you want
to get in, you have to follow the rules. First of all, you have to call
the bar's special reservations number in advance. Then leave a
voicemail or text message with your contact information, wait for
one of the staff to call you back, and last but not least, show up on
time. There are more rules to follow once you get inside; no smoking
(obviously), no telephone calls, no loud voices and no bothering
other patrons. Oddly enough, hats are banned as well. Aside from
the rules, the place is a cozy shelter for conversationalists looking to
enjoy some alcoholic delicacies. The three niches behind the bar are
"illuminated" with an excellent selection of spirits, and the talents of
the bartenders shine both in their re-interpretations of the classics
and in their experimentations on new cocktail horizons. Under the
beautiful coffered tin ceiling, the long bar offers plenty of barstools
where you can sip your cocktail while watching the bar staff ply
their trade. Or you can relax on one of the leather sofas or at a table
with your date or your group of friends. The clientele at Door 74 is a
mix of regulars, customers searching out famous cocktail bars, and
people simply looking to spend a pleasant evening with friends. But
whatever category you may belong to or whoever you choose to
come with, Door 74 is the place for you.

74 Reguliersdwarsstraat, Amsterdam, Netherlands
Telephone: +31634045122
door-74.com

You can't tell a book by its cover.
From the outside, these bars are either invisible
or masquerading as something they are not.
The only way to know the truth is to get inside.

Albert Cuypstraat 129

The

BUTCHER

EST. 2012

1072 CS AMSTERDAM
BURGER BAR

THE BUTCHER

Both the name and the fake bull hanging upside down in the window are clear indications of what to expect inside. In fact, the people who enter The Butcher know exactly what they want. Or do they? It depends on what they know. The window tells you, correctly, to expect a perfect gourmet burger, the best in Amsterdam, but this popular burger bar hides one of the best kept secrets in the city of a thousand canals, provided you know the phone number and password. The door is non-descript and, at first glance, it looks like it might belong to a walk-in freezer, but once you open it, you will find yourself in an elegant, suggestive atmosphere that revolves around a central bar that is usually animated by a crowd of mostly young professionals.

The cocktail menu includes an interesting selection of stimulating punches and drinks created by the resident bartenders and an intriguing choice of recipes made with barrel-aged distilled spirits. If you gain access to the speakeasy, you can also dine in the low light while seated on velvet sofas and taste the meticulously prepared dishes of the "secret" kitchen, beyond its exceptional burgers. The establishment keeps a low profile, owing its success to word-of-mouth, and has a relaxed, intimate ambiance.

The music is low and unobtrusive, ideal for carrying on a conversation while you drink, and only gets more lively in the late evening hours. Officially, the club is only open to members, who are allowed to bring a few guests, but our advice is to call their number (or try flattering the burger chef). It is worth a try.

129 Albert Cuypstraat, Amsterdam, Netherlands
Telephone: +31204707875

JIGGER'S

For a few years after its opening in 2012, Jigger's remained totally invisible from the outside. Only those who knew of its existence could find the door, ring the bell, and be admitted to a perfectly functioning basement speakeasy. But recently things have changed at Jigger's, and the speakeasy has become a bar-within-a-bar. Seen from the street, the venue is a traditional cocktail bar, but downstairs its customary soft lighting, relaxing ambience, and the widespread presence of wood combine to maintain its popularity.

The bartenders at Jigger's like to add a personal twist to their interpretations of the great

16 Oudburg, Ghent, Belgium
Telephone: +3293357025
jiggers.be

classics of mixology. They often use locally sourced garnishes, syrups and infusions which in part accounts for the frequent changes in the drink list.

But the bar is very orthodox in its choices—patrons come here to enjoy a drink in good company, maybe with a bit of background music, but the only drinks they will find on the menu are mixed; wine or beer are not served. It appears to have been the right choice; the bar has won a number of awards for its cocktails and its fame is international. Jigger's also has a small, carefully tended garden for its guests; a suggestive oasis that makes socializing even easier.

CAHOOTS

Soho is London's own crossroads of the world. It is easy to reach and draws millions of tourists that meander through the alleyways of Piccadilly Circus every year. During peak season, which for London is virtually all year round, you can hear almost any language except English. Once famous as the city's red-light district, today Soho teems with theaters, clubs, restaurants and bars that make for a particularly animated nightlife.

Until recently, there was a sign on one of the streets in the neighborhood that read "To the trains". It was the entrance to a former underground station turned into a splendid cocktail bar. Since then, Cahoots has put up a less ambiguous sign, but the bar itself remains a suggestive, semi-secret venue worth discovering. Its underground-themed decor recreates the years immediately after World War II when the tube stations still reminded Londoners of the air raid shelters, but with all the postwar joie de vivre that stemmed from the spirit of victory and newly achieved peace.

The bar is modeled on a train carriage, but fear not, it is not going anywhere. The menu is printed on what resembles an old newspaper, and in it you will find a staggering array of cocktails prepared to perfection with fresh ingredients.

On Saturdays from 1 pm, Cahoots serves their "Squiffy Picnic", an interpretation of afternoon tea featuring cocktails served with sandwiches, sausage rolls, and other typically British treats in classic picnic baskets.

13 Kingly Court, Carnaby, London, United Kingdom
Telephone: +442073526200
cahoots-london.com

CAHOOTS

Cahooch Old Fashioned

2 oz Cahooch Blend (Mount Gay XO Rum,
Bulleit Bourbon, Sweet Vermouth, Cointreau Noir)
4 drops Cahoots Signature Bitters
2/3 oz Izarra
Herbal spray

Swede in the city

1.3 oz O. P. Anderson Aquavit
1/3 oz Izarra Jaune
2/5 oz lemon juice
1/3 oz Fennel extract
1/2 oz Lapsang Souchong syrup
4 Raspberries

EVANS & PEEL

The bar's full name is the Evans & Peel Detective Agency, and its website actually looks
as though it might belong to the likes of Philip Marlowe, the rugged private eye who loved his
cigarettes and liquor, created by Raymond Chandler and masterfully interpreted by Humphrey Bogart
in "The Big Sleep." Even the door looks like it is the entrance to the offices of a private detective,
but in reality it hides a genuine speakeasy on the other side. Certain rules must be followed to
gain entrance, beyond reserving in advance, obviously. Potential patrons must submit a case to be
investigated and then undergo the door staff's interrogation, so a bit of imagination and a pinch
of theatricality are a must.

The speakeasy theme continues on the inside with exposed brick walls, vintage decor and very
soft lighting. Beers are drafted from an old radiator and wine bottles are kept in paper bags that
conceal their content; you never know when police might show up to raid the place. Once you have
settled in to the Prohibition era ambiance, it is time to order. The cocktails are lovingly crafted by
a talented staff of bartenders who use an ample selection of spirits and liquors (including some
rather obscure labels), base ingredients, and homemade syrups and extracts to offer some
interesting twists to classic recipes. You can also dine at Evans & Peel. The food menu includes
US-style small plates that you can pair with a favorite cocktail. Even if the temptation to drink at
least one beer from "the radiator" is truly hard to resist.

310c Earls Court Road, London, United Kingdom
Telephone: +442073733573
evansandpeel.com

CALLOOH CALLAY

Shoreditch used to be just one of the many suburbs that had sprung up around London, but in more recent times it has become a perfectly integrated part of the city and one of its coolest neighborhoods. It bristles with hundreds of bars and restaurants that stay open late, but the one not to miss is the Callooh Callay. One of the first in Shoreditch's renaissance, the bar opened its doors in 2008. It does not look like a speakeasy from the outside, but on the inside the atmosphere is pure vintage.

Soft lighting, designer seating and a splendid hardwood bar give the Callooh Callay the welcoming air of your own living room, assuming of course that you love your own living room. But fantasy and the freedom of expression are also at home here, in a cocktail obviously. The name of the bar is a tribute to Jabberwocky, the nonsense poem written by Lewis Carroll, the author of "Alice in Wonderland". Carroll was full of imagination, and one look at the cocktail list confirms that the same can also be said for the drinks, which are regularly rotated, and the able bartenders. Almond oil, oriental spices and English digestive biscuits are just some of the ingredients that magically appear in the hands of the bartenders. Once a month, they receive a sort of mystery box of specific ingredients they must use to create superb drinks. It tests their professional ability and creativity, but also stimulates the curiosity of Callooh Callay's patrons, who find themselves embarking on a sensorial voyage that has no end.

65 Rivington Street, London, United Kingdom
Telephone: +4402077394781
callohcallaybar.com

The Hackney Carriage

Bulleit Bourbon Whiskey
Stout syrup
Caramel
Lemon juice
Egg white
Licorice
Whiskey Barrel Bitters

129 City Road, London, United Kingdom
Telephone: +442072534101
barnightjar.com

NIGHTJAR

A spectacular, award-winning bar aptly named for a nocturnal bird, the Nightjar, "hides" just off of Old Street in Shoreditch. The atmosphere is warm and welcoming and wood dominates the décor. The coffered ceiling, wood paneled bar, bookcases and vintage novelties make the bar feel a bit like a public drawing room where patrons come to take the edge off of work-day tensions. That may be what has kept the Nightjar classified among the best bars in the world. That and of course the exquisite elegance of their cocktails and the selection of live music they feature every night. But it is most probably a combination of all of these.

The soft lighting is reminiscent of bygone speakeasies and invites quiet conversation— but dancing is also allowed— and the drinks are divided into various themes:

HELEN KANE
Q ♦
SINGER
INSPIRA

NAT KING COLE
K ♥
1919 - 1965
AMERICAN JAZZ PIANIST, VOCALIST;
ACTOR AND TV HOST

DAVE BRUBECK
K ♠
1920-2012
AMERICAN JAZZ PIANIST AND COMPOSER
LEADING PROPONENT OF "COOL JAZZ"

LEAD BELLY
K ♣
1888 - 1949
AMERICAN FOLK & BLUES VIRTUOSO
'KING OF THE 12-STRING GUITAR'

pre-Prohibition, Prohibition, Postwar and Signature. This allows the Nightjar's bartenders, currently headed by Antonio Pescatori, to re-interpret the great classics of cocktails and to unleash their creativity in their own signature drinks. They use exotic, little known herbs and rare spices like sweet osmanthus with its golden yellow flowers and sweet buttery fragrance. Grown in the south of China, its antioxidant qualities made it popular in ancient medicine. Or Devil's claw, a plant with anti-

inflammatory properties that grows in the deserts of Africa, from Namibia to South Africa. But what makes the Nightjar unique is its scrupulous attention to detail in both its cocktails and its atmosphere—the feeling that you have walked into a time machine in the middle of this dynamic English city. Keep your eyes open if you want to find the Nightjar; the address is public, but the bar entrance is half hidden and hard to find among the doors to very normal 24-hour cafes.

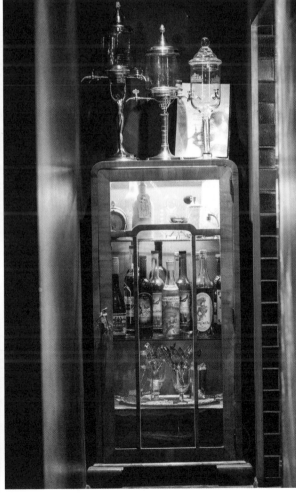

Many modern speakeasies feature live music that is almost always jazz or swing in homage to the Roaring Twenties and the historical period of Prohibition in the United States.

THE BLIND PIG

The Blind Pig was a popular alternative name given to establishments that sold illegal liquor in the United States during Prohibition. It was usually reserved for the most infamous of speakeasies. Soho, which has always been at the heart of London's nightlife, has its own Blind Pig, but there is nothing disreputable about it. It is simply easy to miss as you walk down Poland Street, but despite that fact, its location makes it a well-known haunt among nighthawks. In fact, it is situated above the famed Social Eating House, purveyors of excellent local food, but the Blind Pig is a worthy destination in its own right.

Once you are in the neighborhood, look for a sign that says "Optician". Nearby, you will see a door with a brass doorknocker shaped like a blindfolded pig—a clear indication that you have arrived at your destination.

The bar's wood-rich decor evokes the style and atmosphere of the speakeasies of the 1920s—from the beautiful coffered ceiling to the copper-topped bar, to plush leather sofas and countless mirrors. And if the ambiance reminds you of a gentlemen's club from yesteryear, the pun-filled drink menu will pleasantly surprise you with cleverly-crafted ingeniousness. Children's stories popular all over the world were the inspiration for many of the drinks; the Hunny Pot from Winnie the Pooh, for example. The bartenders at the Blind Pig are true professionals and demonstrate extraordinary creativity in their choice of unexpected ingredients and uncommon presentations.

58 Poland Street, London, United Kingdom
Telephone: +442079933251
socialeatinghouse.com

Dream Jar
Ketel One vodka
Swedish punsch
lemon
orange
vanilla
egg white
thyme essence   10.50

Caen Caen

1.3 oz Calvados Lauriston
2/3 oz Apéritif 30&40
1.3 oz Fresh apple juice
1/2 oz Simple syrup
3 splashes of vanilla bitter
Top off with ginger ale

MOONSHINER

Producing, selling and consuming alcohol were all illegal in the era of Prohibition, but somehow liquor and beer were as readily available as ever. One of the most successful businesses of the period was making "moonshine". Moonshiners distilled spirits usually out of sight, especially the authorities, and under the light of the moon, hence their name. It was hard work that probably did not pay much, but in time it became shrouded in an aura of romance and adventure, which is the image it is associated with today. This is why the words "moonshine" and "moonshiner" sound so good to the ears of an enthusiastic drinker.

As so it is in Paris, where the Moonshiner opened in 2013. Its address is well known, but when you arrive at number 5 Rue Sedaine you might think you have been fooled. Instead of a bar, you will find Da Vito, an Italian food specialty store and pizzeria; but have no fear, all you have to do to gain access to the Moonshiner is flash a big smile at the pizza staff, say "pizzeria" (the password), and push the "secret" door to located in the backroom.

The decor of the Moonshiner is nothing like that of the pizzeria that hides it. The ceiling is covered in finely inlaid wood, exposed brick, and a bar with backlit bottle shelves that alone are enough to make even a teetotaler want a drink. The Moonshiner is home to a selection of about a hundred types of whiskey. The bartenders are constantly at work using a variety of fresh ingredients to produce an endless series of cocktails, but with particular attention to the classics of the 1920s which is no surprise given the bar's Roaring Twenties ambiance.

Early in the evening you can enjoy your cocktail and the atmosphere in total tranquility, but as the night progresses you will be sharing your space, a cocktail, and some conversation with a fascinatingly diversified crowd.

5 Rue Sedaine, Paris, France
Telephone: +33950731299

LITTLE RED DOOR

A door can be a lot of things. It may be a simple door, obviously, but it may also be a passage, a borderline that hides a secret or a mystery on the other side. The poet William Blake wrote: "If the doors of perception were cleansed, everything would appear to man as it is: Infinite". Aldous Huxley also referenced the symbolic role of the door, as did Jim Morrison, the legendary Lizard King, voice and shaman of the famous rock band The Doors. The message in all of this is never to underestimate doors, especially when they're bright red, but also innocent and harmless. In Paris, there is a little red door that will take you, like Alice, into a wonderland for aficionados, a spectacular bar where you can sip phenomenal cocktails. This is what awaits you at the Little Red Door, which opened to the public in 2012.

60 Rue Charlot, Paris, France
Telephone: +33142711932
lrdparis.com

The ambiance is reminiscent of a meticulously restored basement: the walls seem as if in their original state, with exposed brick on one side and white stone on the other. The initial sensation is that of being in a clandestine meeting-place for new recruits or veterans alike: an authentic speakeasy. The twin bars has plush, velvet bar stools ideal for lingering. The bar is a favorite with Parisians, but since its opening has also attracted much attention from an international clientele who spend a few days in Paris. The owners themselves consider it a sort of "hub". The cocktail list has something for everyone: a selection of the classics, always in demand, and an array of creative inventions; all you have to do is ask, preferably with a smile, which around here is always welcome . . . and returned.

51 Rue du Faubourg Saint-Denis, Paris, France
Telephone: +33986262472
syndicatcocktailclub.com

LE SYNDICAT

Don't be fooled by the facade, by the spray-painted graffiti or the many posters that cover it. From the outside you could mistake it for an abandoned building, squatted by urban rebels. This feeling of rebellion is supported by its name, Le Syndicat, and above all is the fact that this place is the headquarters of the Organization for the Defense of French Spirits. As you would expect, the spirits here are the kind you drink. Once inside, you will find yourself immersed in a suggestive atmosphere with long curtains as the barmen work feverishly to craft perfectly balanced potions. The bar's motto is "Organisation de defense des spiritueux francais". In fact, they only serve French liquors.

The ceiling is covered with sound-absorbing material, which gives it the feel of a "revolutionary den". Open seven days a week from 6 pm till two in the morning, Le Syndicat lives kind of a double life depending on which side of the door you are on. Its patrons officially recognize it as a speakeasy and in fact, from the outside it is difficult to imagine what lies beyond the entrance. The founders, Romain Le Mouellic and Sullivan Doh, refer to the bar as a chameleon, capable of camouflaging and hiding itself in a working-class neighborhood; it does not draw attention to itself. But the way it is defined has little importance here. To gain access, there are no passwords or code phrases, and you're not asked secret questions. You just have to remember the saying "you can't tell a book by its cover" and focus on the good vibes that surround the place . . . together with the posters and spray paint.

Le Vieil Hexagone

1 oz French Genever
1 oz Marc de Bourgogne
2/3 oz Izarra
2/3 oz French Vermouth
a splash of absinthe

• Mix ingredients in a mixing glass and serve.

30 Rue René Boulanger, Paris, France
lavomatic.paris

LAVOMATIC

Lavomatic is, without a doubt, the most inviting laundromat in the world. It is fully deserving of this title, as close inspection of the coin-operated washers and dryers will reveal the right button to push, not to wash your dirty laundry, but to open the secret door that opens onto one of the best hidden bars in Paris. Lavomatic opened in 2015 and immediately became a favorite among the city's nighthawks.

The bar's entrance and its cover are original, as is its simple, tastefully furnished interior with the feel of a normal apartment where friends stop by for a cocktail or a glass of organic wine. And the cocktails are just as striking as the decor.

Nothing is prepared ahead of time; rather, everything— syrups, infusions and extracts—is homemade and goes into well-studied combinations of ingredients to make perfectly crafted, original cocktails.

The well-lit and colorful bar is located upstairs, and with such details as stools shaped like detergent boxes you feel as if you are relaxing at a friend's house carefree and casually. The clientele are extremely diversified, but whose common ground is a passion for natural ingredients and products; and these are precisely the basis of the barmen's trade. What we know for sure is that every neighborhood laundromat should be like Lavomatic.

Detoxomatic

Hendrick's Gin
Pineapple juice
Beet juice
Aloe Vera juice
Goji berries
Egg white
Beet root, cumin and Sichuan pepper

QUAND ON VA AU CINÉMA, ON
LÈVE LA TÊTE. QUAND ON REGARDE
LA TÉLÉVISION, ON LA BAISSE.

JEAN-LUC GODARD

PARADISO

One of the best things about the Paradiso is that there is more than one way to enjoy it.
Some passers by stop to savor a pastrami sandwich, and others open the wide refrigerator door
and step into the warm, wood decorated atmosphere of a speakeasy in sharp contrast with the white
tiled walls of the deli outside. The originality of the bar is reflected in the warmth of its decor.
The ceiling and walls are lined with wooden slats that give the impression of being inside something
alive like a huge prehistoric animal, the bottle rack is a tribute to the American Bar at the Savoy of
London, and the bar counter is Carrara marble. The cocktails, handily crafted by the Italian Giacomo
Giannotti, demonstrate professional know-how, creative flair, and a strong desire to astonish. An eye
for aesthetic detail makes their signature cocktails veritable works of art, sometimes seasoned with
a pinch of amusing provocation.

Paradiso has everything it takes to be a must-see on the list of Catalan attractions. That the bar
has been a hit from the time it opened on December 17th, 2015 is no surprise. Secrecy and word
of mouth, the renown of Giannotti—who was awarded best cocktail mixologist in Spain in 2014—
together with the best pastrami in the city combine to make the place worthy of its name— Paradiso.
To savor the exquisite cocktails within, all you need to do is open the right "door" . . . to Paradise,
heaven, that is.

4 Carrer de Rera Palau, Barcelona, Spain
Telephone: +34933607222
paradiso.cat

Mediterranean Treasure

Vodka Ketel One
Sherry infused with
 oyster leaf
Elderflower liqueur
Lemon juice
Mediterranean honey
Coriander leaf
Egg white

• Shake then strain and serve in a shell rimmed with smoked sea salt alongside culinary-torched Mediterranean herbs such as thyme and rosemary.

*So do not be surprised
if your order arrives in a
perfect glass reproduction of
a pipe or in a seashell or an
egg-shaped container . . .*

A BRIEF SPEAKEASY GLOSSARY

   Some terms have been almost completely forgotten, others have been broadened to include new usages and still others have been "resuscitated". In any case, here is a brief list of terms and figures of speech that were popular during the era of Prohibition.

Blind Tiger: or Blind Pig, was one of the names given to establishments that sold illegal alcohol.

Bootlegger: The term was apparently coined during the American Civil War to define soldiers who stole alcohol from the supply cabinets and hid it in their clothing or boots. During Prohibition, the name came to mean anyone who dealt in illegal alcohol.

Dry Crusade: Another way to describe the Temperance Movement and the ideals and actions of those organizations and individuals who fought in favor of Prohibition.

Ginger Jake: One of the most famous and dangerous homemade cocktails of Prohibition, it was often prepared in the bathtub by mixing Jamaican Ginger with triorthocresyl phosphate (TOCP), a chemical element used in hydraulic liquids, lubricants and flame retardants. Research reports that Ginger Jake was responsible for about twenty thousand cases of paralysis during the 1920s.

Hooch: Any kind of illegal liquor.

I have to go see a man about a dog: This was an idiom used to indicate that one had to leave. During Prohibition it came to mean that one was going out to buy alcohol.

Juice Joint: Another name for speakeasies and, by extension, night clubs. It was very popular in the 1920s.

Moonshine: A generally low-quality distillate made with cereal grains (usually corn) that was produced illegally during Prohibition. The name derives from the fact that the clandestine distillers, in an attempt to avoid getting caught, often worked at night under the "light of the moon".

Roaring Twenties: The decade that was marked by Prohibition in the United States went down in history as the "Roaring Twenties", a period of great creativity, liberty and a lust for life. Ten years distinguished by the explosion of jazz music, the affirmation of the Art Deco movement, the normalization of political relations immediately following the end of World War I, and the inception of the first feminist movements (equal voting rights were given to American women in 1920 and British women in 1928).

Rumrunner: The first rumrunners smuggled contraband rum from the Bahamas to sell in Florida speakeasies. Later on, the name was used to identify any illegal alcohol traffickers. Sometimes used as an alternative to bootlegger, the term rumrunner usually referred to smugglers who used boats, whereas bootleggers ran their contraband by land.

Scofflaw: A word used for anyone who drank alcohol, in speakeasies or elsewhere, despite the ban imposed by Prohibition.

Snorky: Slang used to characterize someone who dressed with elegance and attention to detail. Only Al Capone's closest friends dared to use this word to describe him.

Teetotaller: In the 1920s, they were known as teetotalists. Both terms are still used to identify someone who has always observed or has converted to a complete abstinence from alcohol. The list of famous teetotalers is long and includes the astronaut Buzz Aldrin, the world champion boxer Muhammad Ali, the rock star Eric Clapton and the actor Tom Cruise to name a few.

Tight: Slang for someone who is drunk. Synonyms include bent, fried, rummy and zozzled among others.

Wet: A term that indicated an association or party that fought against Prohibition and, by extension, any person that belonged to it.

MY SPEAKEASIES

BIOGRAPHIES

Maurizio Maestrelli. Professional journalist and author, Maurizio Maestrelli has been writing about the world of alcoholic beverages for over twenty years. He has a decided preference for beers and spirits. His articles have appeared in "Il Mondo della Birra", "Gambero Rosso", "Dove", "Economy" and the trade magazine of the Italian Association of Sommeliers of the Lombardy Region. He has written a number of books dedicated to beer, the last of which is "Thomas Hardy's Ale: The Story, The Legend", and he collaborated with Stephen Beaumont and Tim Webb on "The Pocket Beer Book". This, his latest book, is the author's first journey into the world of cocktails, which he wrote with an Old Fashioned always within reach.

Samuele Ambrosi is the owner and head barman at the Cloakroom Cocktail Lab in Treviso, Italy and an advisor for AIBES, The Italian Association of Bartenders. In 2004 he won the national Angelo Zola Competition, and then continued up the ladder winning the Eagle Award in Singapore in 2005, as well as the South Asian Competition in the same year. In 2008 he was awarded the International Calvados Trophy in Normandy. He is currently an instructor for the AIBES and the Campari Academy, as well as a consultant for a number of businesses in the field. Ask him any question you might have about gin—he knows the answer.

ACKNOWLEDGMENTS

A good author knows that every book is conceived with the support of other people. Here, I would like to thank three in particular: Laura Accomazzo, simply because she chose me and especially because, as my editor, she never created anxiety, something rare in her profession; Samuele Ambrosi, who rekindled my passion for cocktails and was an infinite source of information and fun facts about this fascinating, complex topic; and finally, Valentina, my wife, associate and colleague who instills in me the constancy I need to take my projects to the finish line.

Last but not least, I want to thank all of the many bartenders I met with and listened to during my work on this book. You condense emotions into a glass and, for this, I will always be grateful.

The Author

PHOTO CREDIT

WHITE STAR PUBLISHERS

WS White Star Publishers® is a registered trademark
property of White Star s.r.l.

© 2018 White Star s.r.l.
Piazzale Luigi Cadorna, 6 - 20123 Milan, Italy
www.whitestar.it

Translation: Iceigeo, Milan (Cynthia Anne Koeppe, James Schwarten, Lorenzo Sagripanti, Chiara Schiavano)

ISBN 978-88-544-1312-2
1 2 3 4 5 6   22 21 20 19 18

Printed in Italy by Rotolito S.p.A. - Seggiano di Pioltello (Milan)